A Photographic Guide to
BIRDS
OF BRITAIN AND EUROPE

Paul Sterry and Jim Flegg

Connaught

This edition published in 2004 by Connaught
an imprint of New Holland Publishers (UK) Ltd

Garfield House, 86-88 Edgware Road
London W2 2EA
www.newhollandpublishers.com

ISBN 1 84517 035 0

Editor: Charlotte Fox
Designed and typeset by D & N Publishing, Hungerford, Berkshire.
Cartography by Carte Blanche, Basingstoke, Hampshire.

Reproduction by Chroma Graphics, Singapore
Printed and bound in Malaysia by Times Offset (M) Sdn Bhd

Front cover photograph: Kingfisher (Paul Sterry)
Back cover photograph: Puffin (Paul Sterry)
Title page photograph: Redstart (Colin Carver)

Photographic Acknowledgements
All the photographs in this book were supplied by Nature Photographers
Ltd. Most were taken by Paul Sterry, the exceptions being the following:
T. Andrewartha 63ur; F.V. Blackburn 46ul, 49ur, 49lr, 50ul, 96ul, 93ur,
95lr, 96ul, 97ur, 115ur, 117lr, 123lr, 127ur, 180ur; Mark Bolton 110ll;
Derek Bonsall 62ul, 85ur, 98ul, 117ur, 119lr, 125lr; L.H. Brown 26ul;
Kevin Carlson 20ll, 21lr, 24ll, 25lr, 43ur, 54ul, 73ur, 91ul, 94ul, 95ur,
98ll, 101ur, 101lr, 102ll, 104ll, 113ur, 114ul, 114ll, 115lr, 119ur, 120ll,
134ll; Colin Carver 58ul, 104ul, 105ur, 108ul, 112ul, 113lr, 116ll, 121lr,
126ur, 126ll, 130ul, 138ll; Hugh Clark 96ll, 116ul, 118ul; Andrew
Cleave 67lr, 76ul, 76ll; A.K. Davies 124ul; R.H. Fisher 87lr; C.H.
Gomersall 14ul; Michael Gore 46ll, 47ur, 47lr, 87ur, 121ur, 122ll; James
Hancock 91lr; M.R. Hill 65lr, 94ll; E.A. Janes 15lr, 33ur, 41ll, 45lr,
53ur, 54ll, 71lr, 88ul, 107ur, 128ul, 130ll; John Karmali 72ur; Chris &
Jo Knights 79ur; Philip J. Newman 16ul, 51lr, 52ul, 60ll, 88ll, 92ul, 97lr,
109lr, 112ll, 120ur; Wiliam S. Paton 44ul, 48ll; J.F. Reynolds 71ur;
J. Russell 132ul; Don Smith 89ur; Robert T. Smith 16ll, 103ur, 111lr;
E.K. Thompson 14ul; Roger Tidman 20ul, 38ll, 42ul, 44ll, 52ll, 68ul,
70ll, 79lr, 80ul, 84ll, 85lr, 89lr, 93lr, 111lr, 134ul, 135ur, 137lr.

u = upper, l = lower, m = middle, ul = upper left, ur = upper right,
ll = lower left, lr = lower right.

Contents

Introduction

Birdwatching is now one of the most popular outdoor pursuits both in Britain and also in the rest of Europe. The popularity of birds clearly stems from the intrinsically endearing appearance of most species, but other factors contribute as well. Compared with other groups of animals, birds are far more numerous and varied; they also have the advantage of being, in the main, easy to observe well, especially with the aid of modern-day binoculars and telescopes.

As with other endeavours and pastimes, the level of interest and knowledge varies tremendously throughout the birdwatching community. For some people, watching the avian goings-on at the back-garden bird feeder or on the lawn provides hours of entertainment and interest; even without leaving the boundaries of your own garden, a surprising range of species and behaviours can be observed.

Far more people, however, get out and about and visit different habitats on a regular basis: weekend birdwatching makes a fascinating pursuit on its own but adds variety and interest to a family trip to the coast, for example. There are also those who dedicate their lives to the study of birds, either on a part-time or full-time basis, ringing birds to study migration and movement or surveying population numbers.

Lastly, there are the fanatical few who add spice to their birdwatching lives by chasing after new and ever-rarer sightings. The growing army of dedicated 'heavy birders' or 'twitchers' mirrors the increasing interest in birds throughout the population as a whole.

More than 500 species of birds occur in Europe on a regular basis. A book of this size could not hope to provide a comprehensive review of this range, nor does it pretend to do so. In preparing the selection of species for this title, I have included both species that are common and widespread as well as those that are distinctive and representative of specific regions of Europe. In this way, birdwatchers will be able to identify all the common birds on their 'home patch' and also feel at home when visiting different areas on holiday.

The geographical area covered by the book extends from Britain and Scandinavia in north-west Europe, south-west to the Iberian peninsula and south-east to Greece and European Turkey.

The bulk of the book is devoted to bird identification with each species in the book having a representative photograph accompanied by informative text to assist in the process of recognition. However, there are also sections on bird structure, a glossary giving details of ornithological terms, and text on how to identify birds and the more practical aspects of birdwatching in the field. A selection of suggested books to read and useful addresses is included at the back of the book.

How to use this book

The species included in the guide are arranged according to the widely accepted order followed in most other field guides to birds and more general books on the subject.

The photographs
Each species included in the book is accompanied by at least one colour photograph. Considerable thought has gone into the selection of these photographs, the aim being to provide the most useful shot for identification purposes. With some birds, males and females are identical and so identification from the photograph will present no problems. With a few species, however, males and females have different plumages and these can even vary according to the time of year.

The species descriptions
The descriptions provide detailed information on each species included in the guide. They include the following information:

Common name – in all cases, the most popular and widely accepted vernacular English name is used.

Scientific name – each species has a unique scientific name recognised the world over in any language. For example, to a French birdwatcher, a robin is a 'rouge-gorge' but in all languages its scientific name is *Erithacus rubecula*.

Length – this is the distance between the tip of the bill and the tip of the tail.

Appearance – in the text, reference is made to features and plumage details appropriate to the species in question.

Flight – because birds are often seen in flight, it is important not to omit this aspect in their descriptions. Where relevant, the size and shape of the wings is made reference to, as are colours and patterns.

Behaviour – each species of bird has behaviour patterns unique to its kind. These govern aspects of day-to-day life such as feeding, courtship, response to predators and whether the bird is solitary or gregarious.

Habitat – generally speaking, birds are faithful to a particular habitat – one where all their daily needs such as food, shelter and protection, can be obtained.

Voice – voice can be extremely important in identification. Among the passerines – the so-called 'perching birds' or 'song birds' – diagnostic songs are often delivered at the start of the breeding season. A much wider variety of birds, including the passerines, have distinctive calls and experienced birdwatchers can identify a high proportion of common birds by sound alone.

Abundance – all the birds in this guide are common at least somewhere within their European range.

Maps – maps provide concise and easily accessible information about the range of each species. Yellow areas show summer migrants' breeding ranges, blue shows winter ranges and green indicates a year-round presence.

Corner tabs – these provide an at-a-glance reference relating to the species family groups. See key below.

 Divers and Grebes

Tube-noses, Gannets & Cormorants

Pelicans, Herons & allied birds

Swans, Geese & Ducks

Birds of Prey

 Gamebirds

Moorhen & related birds

 Waders

 Skuas, Gulls & Terns

Auks

 Pigeons & Doves

Swift & Nightjar

Owls

Kingfisher & allied birds

Woodpeckers

Cuckoo

Larks

Swallow & Martins

Pipits & Wagtails

Shrikes, Waxwing, Oriole & Starling

 Crows

Dipper, Wren & Dunnock

 Warblers

Flycatchers

Wheatears, Chats & Thrushes

Tits

Nuthatch & Treecreeper

Sparrows, Finches & Buntings

Glossary

Axillaries Underwing feathers at the base of the wing forming the so-called 'armpits'.

Coverts Feathers on the upper and lower surfaces of the wing that assist streamlining in flight.

Eye-stripe Tract of feathers that runs through the eye.

Flight feathers Feathers used for flight; the outer primaries and the inner secondaries of the wings.

Irruption Mass movement of a population from one area to another, usually in response to the exhaustion of food supply.

Juvenile A young bird in its first full plumage.

Lek Communal display area used by males of certain species such as black grouse and ruff.

Mantle The feathers on the back.

Migration The movement by some species from one area to another, the two regions being well defined and their occurrence predictable.

Moult Because feathers become worn and damaged, they are shed regularly and replaced by new ones.

Passage migrant A migrant bird that is seen when it stops off to rest and feed while migrating from its breeding grounds to its wintering quarters.

Passerine A large and extensive group of birds also known as the perching birds because of this ability.

Plumes Long, showy feathers often acquired at the start of the breeding season and used for display.

Race Populations of the same species are sometimes isolated geographically such that they seldom encounter one another and have subtly different plumages. These are described as races.

Raptor A term applied to diurnal birds of prey.

Resident Present within an area throughout the year.

Species Individuals belong to the same species if they are capable of breeding and producing viable offspring.

Speculum Shiny area of feathering on the secondary feathers of the wings of many ducks.

Summer plumage The plumage acquired at the start of the breeding season.

Supercilium The tract of feathers that runs above the eye and eye-stripe as a discrete stripe.

Tube-noses A group of seabirds that includes petrels, shearwaters and fulmars.

Wader A group of birds often with long legs and bills, including sandpipers, plovers and curlews.

Wildfowl The family of birds comprising swans, geese and ducks.

Wingspan The length from one wingtip to the other when fully stretched in flight.

Winter plumage The plumage seen during the non-breeding winter months.

Bird structure and appearance

Even within Britain and Europe, the different species of birds vary tremendously both in terms of size and shape. Despite the apparent dissimilarity between say a goldcrest and a white stork, both these two species, and all others, have many features in common. The basic plan of the skeleton will be essentially the same; even the layout of the plumage will be similar, the feathers growing in tracts which all birds have in common.

A bird's feathers serve a variety of different functions. The most obvious of these have to do with flight. The primaries and secondaries on the wings provide much of the power needed for flight while the coverts on the wings and the contour feathers on the body aid streamlining and an aerodynamic shape.

Feathers also serve to provide the insulation needed to maintain the bird's body temperature and are assisted in this by the underlying down feathers on the body. Lastly, the feathers are often coloured, the patterns produced providing camouflage in some species and colourful display in others.

The illustration shows a stylised line drawing of a typical bunting. The feathered areas of the head can be clearly seen as can the feather tracts of the wings when held at rest. In the posture, of course, some of the wing feathers are partially concealed. The relative lengths of the different feathers and the presence or absence of features such as wingbars on particular tracts of feathers can be important in identification.

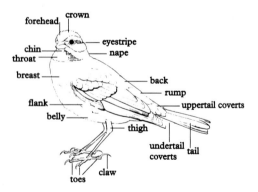

Study the illustration and try to memorize the names and locations of the most important parts of the bird's body. Feather tracts are often represented by discrete blocks of colour which can vary from species to species or according to seasonal plumage. A knowledge of this feathering will enable you to make direct comparisons between species and refer more easily to the descriptions in the text.

Identifying birds

Identifying birds can sometimes be a rather frustrating business, especially for the beginner. When seen by seasoned observers and under ideal conditions, most of the birds in this book should be readily identifiable; birdwatchers new to the pastime may have difficulty under some circumstances. Reassuringly, your ability will without doubt improve over the years and you should be comforted by the knowledge that, however experienced the birdwatcher, there will always be some sightings that defy identification!

Like everything else in life, your birdwatching skills will improve with time and experience. Here are some of the important aspects of birdlife and birdwatching on which to concentrate.

Size
Measuring the length of a bird in the field is clearly not an option in most cases and so the birdwatcher must learn to gauge size. This is not always as easy as it sounds since optical aids – binoculars and telescopes – can often distort the apparent size. Try to compare the bird in question with a nearby individual of known species or an object of known size, remembering to make allowances for foreshortening in perspective if the two are not in the same plane of focus.

Shape
Birds of particular family groups often share distinctive shapes. For example, herons and egrets are, by and large, long-legged and long-necked birds while plovers have short, stubby bills, dumpy bodies and longish legs.

The overall shape of the body and the relative sizes of the head, bill and legs are obviously important. Note should also be made, however, of the bird's stance and posture. Some birds perch and sit upright while others adopt a more horizontal posture; non-perching birds also have a range of postures and stances and it should not be forgotten that these can vary according to the behaviour of the bird.

Colour
When identifying a new bird, make careful observations of the patterns and colours of the plumage. Lighting can be crucial in the observation of colour so take this into account.

It should also be borne in mind that a bird's plumage can vary according to the time of the year and the sex of the individual. Try to be sure whether you are looking at a bird in breeding plumage or a non-breeding bird in winter plumage. Juveniles, which often have cleaner looking feathering in the autumn than adults, are invariably different in appearance from their parents.

Behaviour

The behaviour of a bird can give vital clues to its identification although a degree of patient observation may be needed to discern the more important patterns. Watch, for example, the way in which the bird feeds, whether on the ground or among foliage, or its flight pattern and response to others of the same or different species.

Habitat

Each species is perfectly adapted to feed in a characteristic way in a particular habitat and, only under exceptional circumstances, will it be found elsewhere. There are of course species which are exceptions to the rule, however, with most bird species, a knowledge of their habitat preferences can greatly improve the chances of being able to find them.

Voice

When it comes to a knowledge of bird songs and calls, there is no substitute for field experience. Most birdwatchers will eventually learn all the more common and widespread species given sufficient time. This can be a very satisfying achievement and, at the very least, provides you with a basis upon which to make comparisons when dealing with unfamiliar calls.

Jizz

In many ways the 'jizz' of a bird is a combination of all the above features and aspects, seen through eyes of an experienced birdwatcher. Given years of observation, some people can identify birds even in poor light and at a considerable range. Clues used might be the flight pattern of a speck on the horizon or the feeding pattern of a distant wader far out on the mud flat. At least part of the skill, however, derives from having the background knowledge to make a 'best guess' at the most likely species in a particular habitat at a certain time of year.

Going birdwatching

Having familiarized yourself with the layout of the guide, it is now time to go birdwatching. Although at the simplest level, all you need is a pair of eyes, a certain amount of expenditure on equipment can greatly increase the pleasure derived from the pursuit. Also, the development of fieldcraft skills and a knowledge of when, where and how to watch birds can enhance the experience.

Equipment

A pair of binoculars is part of the uniform of every birdwatcher (along with muddy boots and a set of waterproof clothing). It goes without saying that the more you spend, the better the quality of the binoculars and there are numerous models on the market with price tags that range from under £50 to nearly £1,000. However, you do not necessarily have to spend a fortune to acquire a good pair so go to a reputable dealer and try a few out before you make a purchase.

You will find that all binoculars are accompanied by a set of numbers which give clues as to their value to the birdwatcher. A typical pair might have the numbers 8 × 40 on the casing. The first number is the magnification of the optics and the second is a measure of the light-gathering capacity of the lens and hence the brightness of the image. Do not be tempted into purchasing anything with a magnification of more than 10 or less than 7. The second number should not be less than 30 or the image will be too dark, nor perhaps more than 10 since the binoculars may be too heavy to hold still.

The best advice when buying a pair of binoculars would perhaps be to purchase the ones that feel best to you. The same goes for telescopes which nowadays also come in all shapes and sizes. With a telescope you also need a tripod to stand it on for prolonged observation: the dedicated birdwatcher soon becomes laden with all sorts of paraphernalia!

When and where to go birdwatching

Time of day, time of year and weather all have important influences on the variety and numbers of birds in a given habitat. Before planning an outing that involves any travel, it is often wise to sit and consider your options before you set out.

Habitats offer differing birdwatching opportunities throughout the year. Woodlands, for example are often at their best in the spring when territorial birds are in full song and the leaves are not fully open. Although good throughout the morning, arrive as early as you can after dawn for the best chorus. Woodlands in summer are often rather uninspiring for the birdwatcher but, perhaps surprisingly, winter has plenty to recommend it. Mixed flocks of small birds roam the trees and the lack of leaves makes observation easy.

Sooner or later, birdwatchers find themselves lured to the coast. Again, different areas of coast are best at different times of year. Seabird cliffs and other nesting areas are best in spring and summer, while estuaries come into their own in autumn and winter.

Spring and autumn are periods of migration for many species of European birds, heading to and from summer breeding grounds in northern Europe and wintering grounds, often south of the region. These can be extremely exciting times for birdwatchers with most activity occurring, it has to be said, around the coast. The more dedicated among their numbers eagerly study weather forecasts and maps during these seasons: easterly winds carry birds from eastern Europe and beyond into western Europe; southerly winds carry spring migrants north of their usual range; and westerly gales drive migrating seabirds close to the shores of north-west Europe.

Where to go birdwatching in Europe

Almost any unspoilt area in Europe will have plenty of birdlife to interest the observer and most birdwatchers derive immense pleasure from working their own local 'patch'. However, within the range covered by this book there are a few areas that are particularly noteworthy and well worth the effort of visiting. Some of these may be areas where a good range of breeding birds occurs in the summer, or where wintering species gather in large numbers. Others are migration hotspots where an astonishing range of species occurs in spring and autumn. The following are among the more outstanding.

The Shetland Isles – these islands lie 100 miles or so off the north coast of Scotland. Locations such as Hermaness on Unst and the island of Noss harbour some of the finest seabird colonies in Europe; puffins, guillemots, black guillemots, razorbills and kittiwakes are all easily seen between May and July. Great and Arctic skuas breed on moorland areas.

Isles of Scilly – situated to the west of Cornwall, these islands are among the best in Europe for observing autumn migration. Common migrant species occur in very good numbers but the Scillies are renowned for the rare vagrants from America and Asia that turn up on a regular basis in October.

Slimbridge – situated next to the River Severn in Gloucestershire and run by the Wildfowl and Wetlands Trust, the site protects wintering grounds for vast numbers of geese and ducks. The collection of captive birds is also world famous.

La Brenne – an area of wetlands and arable land in central France which harbours large numbers of breeding species. It is also good at migration times.

Camargue – the network of lagoons, marshes and saltpans in the Rhône delta in southern France, is known the world over for its wetland birds. Breeding birds are abundant and flamingos are often seen.

Gibraltar – the distance between Gibraltar in southern Spain and the north African coast is short and many migrant birds such as birds of prey and storks are concentrated here on their travels to and from Europe. March to May and September and October are the best months.

Majorca – the popular tourist destination of Majorca in the Balearics, offers opportunities for observing most of the classic Mediterranean birds plus an excellent range of migrants in spring and autumn.

Neusiedler See – situated close to Vienna in eastern Austria, this immense, reed-fringed lake is a haven for waterbirds, both during the breeding season and also during migration times.

Grossglockner Pass – this high alpine pass between Austria and Italy allows visitors to see most of the species typical of the mountains of southern Europe. It is easily accessible by car, which makes it an extremely popular tourist destination.

Falsterbo – sited at the southern tip of Sweden, Falsterbo is a superb location for watching the daytime migration of a wide range of birds from flocks of songbirds to birds of prey; autumns are particularly rewarding.

13

Red-throated Diver *Gavia stellata* 55cm

This elegant waterbird has a slightly upturned, dagger-like bill which is usually held pointing upwards at an angle. Summer adult has grey head and neck with black and white streaks on hind neck. Red throat patch looks dark in certain lights. Underparts white and back grey-brown with sparse white markings. Winter adult greyish above with white flecks and white underparts. Immature similar to winter adult. Mostly silent but utters cackling calls near nest. Breeds beside moorland pools. Winters in coastal waters. Local breeding species in northern Europe but rare in Britain. More widespread in winter but rarely numerous.

Black-throated Diver *Gavia arctica* 62cm

A bulkier and heavier species than the Red-throated Diver with a dark and robust bill held horizontally. Summer adult has white underparts and black back with bold white markings. Head and nape grey; throat streaked black with central black patch. Winter adult grey-brown above and whitish below. Clear demarcation between white throat and grey nape. Immature resembles winter adult but has pale, scaly markings on back. Wingbeats slower than Red-throated Diver. Mostly silent but utters eerie, wailing song on breeding grounds. Nests on small islands in large, northern lakes. Winters around coasts and occasionally inland on lakes.

Great Crested Grebe *Podiceps cristatus*   45cm

 A slender neck and long, dagger-like bill distinguish this graceful waterbird. Summer adult grey-brown above and white below. Neck white and head conspicuously crested with tufts of chestnut and black. Winter adult generally greyer and only slight indication of crest. Full grown young is striped but immature resembles winter adult. In flight, appears hump-backed, showing conspicuous white patches on whirring wings. Mostly silent but utters guttural croaks near nest. Breeds on large, reed-fringed freshwater lakes and gravel pits where most are year-round residents. Some winter on sheltered coasts, especially during severe weather. Widespread and fairly common.

Little Grebe *Tachybaptus ruficollis*   25cm

 The smallest and dumpiest of the grebes with a short-necked and characteristically tail-less appearance. Summer adult dark brown. Chin and throat rich chestnut; small yellow patch at base of bill. Winter adult drab brown above and paler below. Immature resembles winter adult. Call is a shrill, far-carrying, whinnying trill. Found year-round on slow-moving rivers, canals, lakes, reservoirs and even ditches. Usually associated with areas of ample marginal vegetation; builds floating nest of water plants. During severe winter weather may move to larger ice-free lakes or even coastal waters. Widespread and common.

Slavonian Grebe *Podiceps auritus* 32cm

This small, dumpy-bodied grebe has a longish, slender neck. Bill is small, dark, straight and dagger-like. Eye is red and beady. Summer adult has chestnut underparts and neck with dark brown back. Head relatively large and black with conspicuous, long, orange tuft over each eye. Winter adult black above and white below. Crown black with clear demarcation from white cheeks. Immature resembles pale brown winter adult. Utters low, rippling trill during breeding season but otherwise silent. Breeds on small, vegetated lakes. Rare breeding species in Britain. Winters on coastal seas and occasionally inland.

Black-necked Grebe *Podiceps nigricollis* 30cm

An attractive waterbird, similar to the Slavonian Grebe but with high forehead and round head profile. Bill is noticeably uptilted. Summer adult has black back, neck and head with chestnut flanks. Golden, fan-shaped crest on sides of head. Winter adult greyish above and whiter below, showing gradual shading between. Immature resembles winter adult. During breeding season, utters piping 'peep' call, like young Great Crested Grebe. Breeds on densely vegetated lakes. Very rare breeding species in Britain. Winters on estuaries, lakes and reservoirs. Numbers and distribution variable but seldom common.

Fulmar *Fulmarus glacialis* 45cm

A streamlined seabird with a heavy body. Adult and immature superficially gull-like in appearance and plumage. Pale grey above shading to white below. Wings lack any black. Beak yellowish, with tubular nostrils on ridge. Flies on straight, outstretched wings. Typically, glides extensively with few wingbeats except when close to cliffs. Mostly silent but cackling and crooning calls heard on breeding ledges. Nests colonially on coastal cliffs or on ground on remote islands. Otherwise seen at sea throughout year. Mostly in coastal waters but some disperse to mid-ocean in winter. Widespread and locally common.

Manx Shearwater *Puffinus puffinus* 35cm

A distinctive, well-marked seabird. Adult and immature completely black above and strikingly white below. Recognized in flight when frequent changes in direction reveal alternately flashing black and white. Glides on stiff wings low over waves with minimal wingbeats. Silent at sea but strange cacophony of bubbling and crowing calls heard at breeding colonies. Nests in burrows on remote islands, only visiting land after dark. Very locally common on islands off west coast of Britain such as Skomer. YELKOUAN SHEARWATER (*Puffinus yelkouan*) is similar but browner above. Locally common in the Mediterranean.

British Storm-petrel *Hydrobates pelagicus* 15cm

A tiny seabird with a butterfly-like flight. Adult and immature sooty black. In flight, white rectangular rump patch clearly visible. Wings also show faint, greyish, diagonal bar on upperside and bolder white bar on underside. Tail black, often held in rounded fan, especially when feeding. Beak tiny and dark with tubular nostrils. Silent at sea. During nocturnal visits to breeding colonies, high-pitched purring call heard, with sporadic clicks. Breeds in burrows and crevices on remote rocky islands and cliffs. Occurs far offshore during daytime and winter. Often follows ships for food. Occasionally comes close to land during severe gales. Very locally common at breeding colonies.

Gannet *Sula bassana* 90cm

This huge, distinctive, goose-like seabird plunge-dives spectacularly for fish. Adult largely white with cigar-shaped body and long tail. Long straight, pointed wings. show black tips; head and long neck have yellow tinge. Bill is steel-grey, long and dagger-shaped. First year immature is grey-brown, flecked with white. Gradually acquires more white over next three years. Flight characterized by slow, stiff wingbeats, interspersed with frequent glides. Silent at sea but raucous honks heard on breeding grounds. Nests colonially on remote islands or cliffs. Winters in off-shore waters but sometimes passes close to headlands. Widespread and locally common.

Cormorant *Phalacrocorax carbo* 90cm

A large, long-necked seabird swims low in the water and dives frequently. Adult blackish with metallic sheen. Facial skin yellow. Beak yellow with hooked tip. In summer, shows white patches on face and sometimes thighs. Southern European breeding birds may have head and neck white. Winter adults lack white patches. Immature dark brown above but paler on throat and underparts. Often seen perched on posts with broad wings spread to dry. Mostly silent but guttural grunts heard on breeding grounds. Nests colonially on island and cliffs beside shallow seas or estuaries. Winters mainly around coasts, occasionally on freshwater. Widespread.

Shag *Phalacrocorax aristotelis* 75cm

A large, dark seabird similar to the Cormorant but smaller and slimmer. Summer adult blackish with green iridescent sheen with no white patches. Beak slim and yellow at base with hooked tip. Curled crest in early spring, traces of which persist into summer. Immature brown, appreciably darker-bellied than immature Cormorant. In flight, slighter build, slimmer neck and smaller head help distinguish from Cormorant. Also perches with wings spread to dry. Mostly silent but harsh croaks heard on breeding grounds. Year-round resident on rocky coasts and near to clear seas. Often nests in loose colonies. Locally very common.

Bittern *Botaurus stellaris* 75cm

A large and superficially heron-like bird. Long neck is concealed in normal stance with head held low between shoulders. Adult and immature mainly brown. Copiously streaked and barred with black, chestnut and buff, creating perfect camouflage in reedbeds. Throat is whitish. Beak pale and dagger-like; legs greenish and long. Flight slow, broad-winged, with head retracted. Inconspicuous and shy. Deep, foghorn-like booming heard during breeding season but otherwise silent. Occurs in extensive reedbeds year-round. Northerly populations move southwest in winter. Widespread but local and rare, being restricted by habitat.

Little Bittern *Ixobrychus minutus* 35cm

A small, secretive and rather dumpy heron. Adult rich buff below and brownish-black above. Female plumage more subdued than male. In flight, both sexes show pale buff patches on inner upperwing. Immature brown, streaked black like miniature Bittern, but with clearly visible buff patch on wing. Green legs trail in flight like those of Moorhen. Deep croaking calls heard at intervals day and night during breeding season but otherwise silent. Occurs in densely vegetated swamps and reedbeds. Widespread in Europe as summer visitor but rarely seen because of retiring nature. Rare vagrant to Britain but has bred.

White Pelican *Pelecanus onocrotalus* 160cm

This huge waterbird has broad wings spanning 250cm. Adult largely white. In breeding season, has short, drooping crest, yellowish wash on breast and sometimes an overall pinkish flush. Huge beak is pinkish-grey with yellow pouch. Legs and feet flesh pink. In flight, small amount of black shows on upperwing but broad black band stretches entire length of trailing edge on underwing. Immature buff with brown wings and paler underparts. Guttural croaks heard during breeding season but otherwise silent. Occurs on freshwater swamps and lakes, nesting colonially. Occasionally seen on sheltered coastal seas.

Little Egret *Egretta garzetta* 55cm

A slender, elegant, medium-sized heron. Adult pure white with long, slender neck usually held extended. In breeding season, has long white crest and fine white plumes on back. Beak long, black and dagger-shaped. Legs long and black with striking, yellow feet. Immature whitish, lacking plumes and crest. In flight, head withdrawn between shoulders but legs extended. Various harsh honks and shrieks during breeding season but otherwise mostly silent. Found on freshwater and shallow, sheltered coastal waters. Breeds colonially in trees close to feeding habitat. Locally common in Europe. Increasingly frequent visitor to southern England.

Great White Egret *Egretta alba* 90cm

A huge, pure white heron, much larger than the Little Egret. Adult glossy white with fine white plumes on back during breeding season. Neck long, usually held in angular kinks. Beak yellow in breeding season but yellow and black at other times of year. Legs and feet blackish. Immature less strikingly white with blackish beak. Flight stately, head withdrawn between shoulders, legs extended. A loud, harsh 'aark' is occasionally heard near nest or when alarmed. Occurs in extensive marshes, reed-fringed lakes and saline lagoons. Rather local and scarce throughout Europe and is a very rare vagrant to Britain.

Cattle Egret *Bubulcus ibis* 50cm

This smallish, stocky heron is predominantly white. Summer adult white with crown, throat and plumes on back (during breeding season only) ginger buff. Winter adult white, tinged buff. Beak pinkish-yellow and legs yellow. Immature dull white with grey legs. Heavy, underhung 'chin' is characteristic. Utters harsh calls at breeding colonies but otherwise silent. Nests colonially with other egrets in trees or reedbeds. Usually feeds in drier areas than other egrets, often among cattle or following plough. Locally common in south-west Europe. Vagrant elsewhere in Europe including Britain.

Squacco Heron *Ardeola ralloides*   45cm

A smallish, stocky heron. White wings concealed at rest but striking and characteristic in flight. Summer adult predominantly rich golden buff. Long, trailing crest plumes are brown and white. Beak yellowish with black tip; legs greenish. Winter adult drabber, lacking plumes. Immature buff, streaked dark brown with off-white wings. Harsh heron-like honks and shrieks heard during breeding season but otherwise mostly silent. Occurs in freshwater and brackish marshes, swamps and lagoons. Breeds colonially, often with other egrets, in trees or reedbeds. Locally common in southern Europe. Rare vagrant further north including Britain.

Grey Heron *Ardea cinerea*   90cm

The commonest heron in Europe. Adult blue-grey above, white below. Neck white with dark streak down slender throat. Head mostly white with black stripe through eye. Beak yellow, heavy and dagger-like. Breeding adult has drooping black and white crest and long silver-grey plumes on back. Legs yellowish and long. Immature resembles adult, lacking crest and plumes. In flight, head retracted and legs extended. Flight stately on broad wings, blackish primaries contrasting with otherwise grey wings. Harsh shrieks when breeding, otherwise mostly silent. Occurs in all wetlands. Breeds colonially in trees or reedbeds. Widespread.

23

Night Heron *Nycticorax nycticorax* 60cm

This is a rather stout-bodied, short-legged heron with a thick neck and a short, thick bill. It is most active at dusk and roosts during the day. Adult white below with pale grey wings. Crown and back dark grey. When breeding, has long, trailing, white crest plumes. Beak and legs yellowish. Immature buffish-brown with dark streaks and white teardrop markings in rows on closed wings. Flight moth-like. Groups often fly in irregular V-formation. Harsh, heron-like cries when breeding, otherwise silent. Occurs on freshwater and saline marshes, streams and ditches. Nests in mixed egret colonies in waterside trees. Locally fairly common in southern Europe. Rare vagrant as far north as Britain.

Purple Heron *Ardea purpurea* 78cm

A large, slim heron, appearing dark in strong light. Adult dark grey-brown above; chestnut and black below. Neck very long and slender. Nape chestnut; throat white with dark streaks. When breeding, dark purplish crown extends into drooping crest. Back carries fine pale-edged chestnut plumes. Beak yellowish, long and dagger-shaped. Immature rich brown above, paler below. In flight, head retracted, long, greenish-yellow legs extended with hind toe carried erect. Mostly silent. Occurs in reedbeds and other freshwater habitats with abundant emergent vegetation. Nests colonially in reedbeds. Locally fairly common in mainland Europe.

24

White Stork *Ciconia ciconia* 100cm

A huge, unmistakable heron-like bird. Adult white (often dirty white) with extensive black on wings, flight feathers black. Head and neck white. In breeding season, throat feathers shaggy. Beak long, red and dagger-like. Legs long and red. Immature resembles drab adult with brownish beak and legs. Flight slow and stately on broad wings; head and neck carried outstretched. Soars effortlessly. Hisses, grunts and bill-clattering heard at nest but otherwise mostly silent. Feeds in fields and marshes; nests on buildings or sometimes in trees. Sociable. Locally fairly common in south-west and eastern Europe. Rare vagrant to Britain.

Spoonbill *Platalea leucorodia* 82cm

A large and superficially egret-like species but with a long, spoon-shaped bill. Adult white, with yellow at base of neck and drooping yellow-tinged crest in summer. Bill black with yellow tip and legs brownish. Wings white and narrow, pointed in flight, showing black wing tips. Immature dull white with pinkish-grey beak and legs; acks crest. In flight, head and neck held outstretched. Grunting calls heard at nest site, otherwise mostly silent. Occurs in extensive areas of open, shallow water, fresh, brackish or saline. Feeds by sweeping bill from side-to-side. Sociable. Local but rarely numerous.

Greater Flamingo *Phoenicopterus ruber*   125cm

A huge, slim, unmistakable bird. Immensely long neck and wings and proportionately small head and body. Adult has pinkish body and paler neck. Downcurved, banana-shaped, pink bill with black tip. Legs bright pink. Wings startlingly scarlet and black in flight. Immature greyer, paler and slightly smaller. In flight, neck and legs held outstretched, wings appear pointed; often in loose V-formation. Filter-feeds with head down. Utters various goose-like honks and cackles. Occurs in extensive, shallow, brackish lagoons, sometimes in freshwater. Sociable. Very locally common in southern Europe.

Mute Swan *Cygnus olor*   150cm

A huge and unmistakable waterbird. Adult all-white, with long neck carried in graceful 'S' curve. Beak dark orange. Black knob on forehead larger in male than female. Adult raises wings like sails right over back in defence of territory or young. Immature pale grey-buff with pinkish-grey beak. In flight, the long, broad, heavily fingered wings creak loudly. Rarely vocal but hisses or grunts when annoyed. Occurs on all types of freshwater larger than ponds, including town lakes. Occasionally on sheltered coasts, especially in winter. Widespread and common in north-west Europe.

Whooper Swan *Cygnus cygnus* 150cm

A huge swan with a long, straight neck which is carried vertically except when feeding. Adult all-white. Beak black with large, yellow, wedge-shaped patch at base, extending beyond nostrils. Beak lacks basal knob. Immature pale greyish with pinkish markings on beak. Flight steady and powerful on broad, heavily fingered wings. Wingbeats silent. Wild, bugle-like whooping calls uttered frequently in flight or on ground. Breeds on swampy tundra. Winters on coastal grazing marshes and large freshwater lakes. Winter visitors faithful to regular sites. Scarce, but small numbers regularly winter in Britain.

Bewick's Swan *Cygnus columbianus* 120cm

An elegant swan which is appreciably smaller than other swans. Neck relatively short, straight and goose-like. Adult all-white. Wedge-shaped black beak has irregular, individual, yellow patch at base, not extending beyond nostrils. Immature pale grey with greyish- or pinkish-yellow basal patch on beak. In flight, more buoyant with faster wingbeats than its larger relatives. Wingbeats silent. Frequent musical, goose-like honks and chatterings. Family groups often discernible among winter flocks. Breeds on swampy tundra; winters on extensive grazing marshes, sometimes on cultivated land. Rather scarce but locally numerous on regular wintering grounds from October to March.

27

Canada Goose *Branta canadensis*   75cm

A large distinctive goose, which is almost swan-sized. Adult body dark brown above and paler below. Shows white patch below tail. Head and long neck black. Characteristic white face patch on cheeks and under chin. Beak black and legs dark grey. In flight, black rump and white band on black tail are conspicuous. Wings dark brown; wingbeats powerful. Immature similar to adult but duller. Utters hoarse, disyllabic 'ahh-honk'. Introduced to north-west Europe from North America; now well established on freshwater lakes and marshes, and adjacent grassland. Locally common, especially in Britain. Transatlantic vagrants sometimes occur.

Barnacle Goose *Branta leucopsis*   62cm

This small goose has distinctive, pied plumage. Adult has grey back with black and white barring. Rump white and tail black. Wholly white below. Nape and neck black with contrasting white face and throat. Beak stubby and dark grey; legs black. Immature similar to adult. Winter flocks are very vocal, uttering series of puppy-like, yapping calls. Gregarious, breeding on rocky outcrops in tundra. Winter flocks occur on coastal grassland and saltmarsh. Rather rare but locally numerous at traditional wintering sites from October to March. Small groups occasionally occur away from usual locations during severe winter weather.

Greylag Goose *Anser anser* 80cm

The largest and most widespread of the grey geese. Heavily built, adult dark grey-brown above with faint, paler feather fringes. Pale grey-brown below and white undertail. Head and neck dark brown and stout. Large beak is pink in eastern race and orange in western race. Legs pink. Wingbeats powerful and steady, with pale blue-grey forewing patches conspicuous in flight. Immature similar but duller. Extremely vocal, uttering nasal gabbling and honking similar to farmyard geese. Colonial breeder on moorland and tundra, often close to water. Winters on marshes, farmland and estuaries. Locally common feral populations in many areas.

White-fronted Goose *Anser albifrons* 70cm

A medium-sized grey goose. Adult grey-brown with white beneath tail. Breast has heavy, black barring. Head and neck darker brown, with large white face patch at base of beak. Beak pink in eastern or Russian race or orange-yellow in western or Greenland race. Legs orange. Immature similar but lacks white face and breast barring of adult. Noisy, flocks uttering gabbling and yapping calls. Breeds on tundra and winters on rough grassland, coastal grazing marshes and agricultural land. Widespread and very locally numerous at traditional wintering sites from October to March. Flocks occasionally mingle with other wildfowl.

29

Bean Goose *Anser fabilis* 75cm

A large grey goose. Adult dark brownish-grey above and only slightly paler below. White beneath tail. Neck relatively long and very dark brown. Beak long, wedge-shaped, black with variable pattern of small orange-yellow markings. Legs orange-yellow. Immature similar but legs pale yellowish. In flight, wings appear uniformly dark brown. Mostly silent but low, gruff 'ung-unk' call is distinctive. Breeds in open northern forest near water. Winters on damp meadows and marshes, occasionally on arable fields. Uncommon and local, small numbers wintering in eastern England.

Pink-footed Goose *Anser brachyrhynchus* 65cm

A small grey goose. Adult has blue-grey back and dark brown breast and flanks. Shows white beneath tail. Neck relatively short, appearing almost black in strong light. Head dark and small. Short, stubby beak is mostly black with pink markings. Legs pink. In flight, grey back and forewings contrast with dark head and neck. Immature similar or slightly paler. Extremely vocal, uttering characteristic 'wink-wink-wink' call. Breeds on rocky outcrops in tundra. Winters on freshwater marshes, saltmarshes, large lakes and arable land nearby. Local but locally common winter visitor to Britain and adjacent areas of mainland Europe.

Brent Goose *Branta bernicla* 60cm

A small, very dark goose with short-necked appearance. Adult has blackish-brown back and rump. Tail white with black terminal band and white undertail. Head and neck sooty black with small white collar mark. Pale-bellied race *hrota* and dark-bellied race *bernicla*. Beak blackish and small. Legs blackish. Immature lacks collar mark, has pale barring across back. Rapid wingbeats and white tail conspicuous in flight. Flies in irregular, loose flocks, not orderly V-formations. Soft, low 'rruuk' call. Gregarious, breeding on Arctic tundra. In winter, favours coasts and nearby grazing marshes and fields. Widespread and locally common.

Mallard *Anas platyrhynchos* 58cm

The best known and most widespread duck in Europe. Adult male grey-brown, tail white with black above and below. Curled black feathers on rump. Head bottle green, separated from chestnut breast by narrow white neck-ring. Beak yellow-green and legs orange. Female and immature speckled brown, buff and black. Beak brownish-orange. In flight, both sexes show broad purple speculum patch between white bars on inner section of wing. Male utters quiet whistle; female harsh quacks. Occurs year-round on almost any waters, from small ponds to open seas. Common and almost ubiquitous.

male (above)
female (below)

Gadwall *Anas strepera* 50cm

 A medium-large surface-feeding duck. Adult male greyish-brown with fine vermiculations visible at close range. Undertail characteristically black. Both female and immature are speckled brown. In flight, both sexes show distinctive black and white patch on trailing edge of wing. Mostly silent but female produces descending series of 'kaak' quacks. Breeds on freshwater marshes and beside lakes and other large fresh waters. Winters in similar areas, but also on gravel pits and occasionally on sheltered coastal waters. Usually seen in loose flocks outside breeding season. Widespread but seldom numerous.

Pintail *Anas acuta* 70cm

 A large, slim surface-feeding duck. Adult male has white belly, finely marked grey flanks and grey-brown back. Head and long neck rich brown, with distinctive white mark on side of neck. Beak and legs grey. Tail black, long and pointed. Female and immature pale grey-brown with darker markings. Tail short and pointed. Flight silhouette slender and elongated. Wings narrow, inconspicuous brown speculum on trailing edge. Mostly silent; male has low whistle, female a low, quiet 'quack quack' and a churring growl. Breeds close to water on moors and freshwater marshes. Winters on sheltered coastal waters, sometimes inland.

Wigeon *Anas penelope* 45cm

A medium-sized surface-feeding duck. Adult male has finely marked grey back and flanks and black undertail. Breast pink and head chestnut with gold crown stripe. In flight, shows conspicuous white oval patch on wing. Female and immature similar with cinnamon-brown plumage flecked with darker markings and greyish wing patch in flight. Male utters characteristic plaintive whistle, female a low-pitched purr. Breeds close to water on moorland and tundra. Winters on lakes, estuaries and sheltered seas and nearby marshes and grassland. Widespread and often common in suitable habitats.

Teal *Anas crecca* 35cm

The smallest European surface-feeding duck. Adult male predominantly greyish with conspicuous white stripe on flanks and golden-yellow undertail. Breast buff with fine grey barring. Head chestnut with dark green patch around eye. Female and immature speckled grey-brown. Fast, erratic flight. Male utters distinctive, low 'krit' and bell-like whistle. Female utters harsh 'quack'. Breeds on boggy or marshy land with reed-fringed pools. Winters in similar habitats, often well inland. Also frequently found on estuaries and in sheltered coastal waters. Widespread and often common in suitable habitats.

Garganey *Anas querquedula* 40cm

A small, surface-feeding duck. Adult male has white belly, shading to grey on flanks. Back brown but with conspicuous long, grey and white feathers drooping over flanks. Head, neck and breast rich brown. Striking white stripe above and behind eye. Female and immature sandy brown, with darker markings. In flight, both sexes show characteristic pale blue-grey patches on forewing. Flight almost as fast and agile as Teal. Male utters distinctive, crackling rattle; female a short, harsh quack. Breeds on freshwater marshes and reed-fringed lakes. Seen in similar habitats on migration. Widespread summer visitor but seldom numerous.

Shoveler *Anas clypeata* 50cm

A medium-sized surface-feeding duck with a massive, spoon-shaped beak. Adult male brown above, white below, with striking chestnut patches on flanks. Breast white, head and short neck dark bottle green. Beak dark grey. Female and immature speckled brown with orange-brown beak. Swims low in water, head tilted down. In flight, has rapid wingbeats, head-up, tail-down attitude and pale grey forewing patches. Male utters low-pitched, double quack 'tuk-tuk'; female quiet quack. Breeds on marshland with reed-fringed pools or lakes. Winters in similar areas but also on reservoirs and sheltered coastal waters. Common.

Shelduck *Tadorna tadorna* 60cm

This large goose-like duck has striking, pied plumage. Adult predominantly white with bottle green head and neck. Broad chestnut band round base of neck, two long black stripes on back and central black stripe on belly. Beak scarlet, knob at base larger in male than female. Female may have whitish patch at base of beak. Legs pink. Immature grey-brown and mottled with vague adult patterning. Lacks chestnut collar. Utters barking 'ak-ak-ak' and deep, nasal 'ark'. Found on estuaries and sheltered, sandy or muddy coasts. Occasionally on freshwater. May breed far from water. Widespread and locally common.

Red-crested Pochard *Netta rufina* 55cm

A large diving duck but which dives relatively infrequently and behaves more as a surface feeder. Adult male has brown back, black breast and belly and conspicuous white flank patches. Head rich chestnut with paler, golden, erectile crest. Beak bright scarlet. Female and immature dull brown, paler on belly. Crown dark brown, contrasting with characteristic pale grey cheeks. In flight, both sexes show striking broad white band running full length of wing. Call a grating 'kurr'. Found on large, reed-fringed areas of fresh or brackish water. Uncommon and local. Many recorded in Britain may be escapees from captivity.

Scaup *Aythya marila*   45cm

A medium-sized duck which dives frequently. Adult male has grey back with fine vermiculations. Flanks and belly white, head glossy black with greenish sheen. Neck, breast, rump and undertail black. Female dark brown above, paler on flanks, with conspicuous, large, white patch at base of beak. Both sexes' eyes golden-yellow and beaks grey and blacktip. In flight, shows bold white wingbar and characteristic pale grey back in male. Mostly silent; male has crooning whistle, female a harsh, double quack. Breeds near water on marshland. Normally winters on coastal seas, occasionally on gravel pits and reservoirs. Locally common.

Tufted Duck *Aythya fuligula*   43cm

A medium-sized, compact diving duck. Adult male black above with purple sheen to head and drooping crest during breeding season. Breast black, flanks and belly strikingly white. Undertail black. Female and immature dark brown above, paler below, shading to pale grey-buff on belly. Wingbeats rapid with narrow white wingbar running full length of wing. Dives frequently. Mostly silent; male has soft whistle, female a low-pitched growl. Breeds beside reed-fringed ponds and lakes. Winters on similar and larger water bodies. Often seen on reservoirs and gravel pits. Widespread and often locally common.

Pochard *Aythya ferina* 45cm

A medium-sized diving duck. Adult male has grey back. Mostly white below with breast and undertail black. Head dark chestnut. Female and immature are dull rufous-brown, paler on cheeks, throat and belly. Both sexes have characteristic, steeply rising forehead and greyish wings with indistinct, paler grey wingbar. Dives frequently. Often mixes with Tufted Ducks and other wildfowl. Mostly silent; male has hoarse whistle, female a harsh growl. Breeds beside large, reed-fringed freshwater bodies. Winters in similar locations but also on reservoirs and much less frequently along sheltered coasts. Widespread and locally common.

male (above)
female (below)

Ruddy Duck *Oxyura jamaicensis* 40cm

A squat, stiff-tailed duck. Male has reddish-brown upperparts, breast and flanks, shading to white on belly. Crown and head black but face white. Head carried low. Beak and feet blue-grey. Female and immature mottled brown, darker above than below. Crown blackish and cheeks pale buff. Mostly silent. Introduced to Britain from North America and breeding populations now established on freshwater lakes in southern England. WHITE-HEADED DUCK (*Oxyura leucocephala*) is similar but male has white head with black on nape and around eye. Rare and local resident of southern Iberian peninsula.

Goldeneye *Bucephala clangula* 48cm

A medium-sized, diving sea duck. Adult male predominantly black above, white below. Row of large, white patches on closed wing often merge into a bar. Crested, angular head, black with greenish iridescence. Small, circular white patch below eye. Female and immature brown above, slightly paler on flanks, belly white. Head chestnut and angular. Swims buoyantly, usually in small groups, dives frequently. In flight, white wing patches conspicuous in both sexes. Mostly silent; male occasionally utters disyllabic, nasal call, female a harsh growl. Breeds in hollow trees near water. Winters on coasts or large freshwater lakes. Seldom numerous.

Long-tailed Duck *Clangula hyemalis* 50cm

A small-bodied, long-tailed sea duck. Summer adult male largely dark brown but with cheeks and flanks white. Tail very long and black. Winter male largely white with brown face patches and blackish breast and back. Summer female brown above and white below with white face patches. Tail shorter than male and pointed. Winter female and immature have more extensive white on head and neck. Swims buoyantly and dives frequently. In flight, its small size and pied appearance are characteristic. Vocal, with varied, high-pitched, goose-like honks. Breeds on tundra and winters in coastal seas. Locally common, rarer in south.

Velvet Scoter *Melanitta fusca* 55cm

A large, heavily built sea duck. Adult male uniform black but with small white eye-patch (usually visible only at close range) and white patch on wing (usually concealed in closed wing). Beak yellow with black margins. Female and immature dull brown above, paler below, with buffish, smudgy face patches. Swims buoyantly and dives frequently. In flight, both sexes show characteristic, bold white trailing edge to inner section of wing. Rarely vocal, occasionally utters whistles or growls. Breeds beside rivers and lakes, on tundra and in northern forest fringes. Winters at sea, often in company of Common Scoter. Seldom numerous.

Common Scoter *Melanitta nigra* 50cm

A medium-sized, heavily built sea duck. Adult male unique among ducks with uniformly velvet black plumage. Beak heavy, black and yellow, with black knob in breeding season. Female and immature dull brown, paler below. Buffish face patches contrast with brown crown. Dives frequently. Flocks characteristically fly in long, straggling lines, low over sea, showing uniformly dark wings. Male utters various crooning calls, female utters harsh growls. Breeds beside moorland lakes and on tundra beside rivers. Winters at sea. Rather scarce breeding species in Europe; very local and rare breeder in Scotland and Ireland. Widespread and locally common winter visitor.

Eider *Somateria mollissima* 60cm

male (above)
female (below)

This stocky sea duck has a heavy, wedge-shaped beak. Adult male has white back and black flanks, belly, rump and tail. Breast white, tinged pink when breeding. Head and neck white, black patch across forehead and through eye. Cheeks greenish when breeding. Young males dark, becoming whiter through series of pied plumages. Female brown with dark barring. Flight laboured and low over sea. Female shows faint, white wingbar. Male shows contrasting white back and black flight feathers. Flocks, diving frequently. Male has loud, moaning call, female a grating 'coorrr'. Breeds on coasts and islands. Winters around coasts. Widespread and locally common.

Smew *Mergus albellus* 40cm

male (above)
female (below)

The smallest and most compact of the sawbill ducks. Adult male unmistakable. Predominantly white with fine black lines and grey vermiculated flanks. Crest erected when excited. Female and immature grey-brown, darker above than below. Crown reddish-brown, contrasting with white face. In both sexes, beak grey and slim, with serrated edge. In flight, both sexes show conspicuous white patches on inner sections of wing. Mostly silent. Breeds in hollow trees or ground cavities close to freshwater on tundra. Winters on large freshwater lakes, also occasionally on reservoirs and flooded gravel pits. Widespread but local and rarely numerous.

Goosander *Mergus merganser* 63cm

The largest sawbill duck, with a long, red beak. Adult male has white breast, flanks and belly, with pink flush early in breeding season. Appears very white at a distance. Back black; head bottle green, angular in silhouette because of drooping crest. Female and immature have grey back and pale grey flanks shading to white on belly. Breast and throat white; head and neck chestnut, with neat, drooping crest. Swims low , diving frequently. In flight, shows white wing patches. Usually silent. Nests in hollow trees close to lakes and rivers. Winters mainly on large fresh waters. Widespread but seldom numerous.

Red-breasted Merganser *Mergus serrator* 55cm

A medium-sized sawbill duck with a narrow, red beak. Adult male has black back, finely marked grey flanks and considerable white on closed wing. Lower neck and belly white with broad, chestnut breast band, speckled darker. Head, ragged crest and neck, dark with green sheen. Female and immature grey above, paler buffish-grey below. Head and nape chestnut-brown, with ragged, spiky crest. Both sexes appear elongated on water and in flight, with conspicuous black and white wing patches. Swims low, diving frequently. Mostly silent. Breeds in holes beside rivers and streams. Winters mostly along sheltered coasts. Widespread but seldom numerous.

Griffon Vulture *Gyps fulvus* 105cm

The most typical European vulture. Huge size, adult sandy-brown with slightly paler breast and sometimes streaked. Head and neck pale grey, covered in short down, with whitish ruff around shoulders. Beak massive and hooked. Legs grey and talons weak. Immature browner, with pale feather fringes giving scaly appearance to back; brown ruff at base of neck. Soars effortlessly on broad, heavily fingered wings, the head appearing relatively small. Flight feathers and short tail appear dark. Circles on thermals and flocks at carrion. Mostly silent except for occasional hisses and grunts. Occurs in remote mountain country in warm regions. Seldom common.

Golden Eagle *Aquila chrysaetos* 83cm

A huge and majestic eagle. Adult uniformly rich dark brown, with golden tinge to head and nape. Beak massive and hooked. Immature has characteristic white patches on wings and white tail with broad black terminal band. White areas get smaller with age. Impressively long, broad, heavily fingered wings held slightly above the horizontal when soaring, but with tips often curled downwards. Tail comparatively long and broad. Mostly silent but barking 'kaah' occasionally heard. Occurs in remote mountain and forest areas, down to sea level in places. Widespread but never common. In Britain, confined mainly to Highland region and western Scotland.

Booted Eagle *Hieraaetus pennatus* 48cm

A buzzard-sized eagle, occurring in two colour forms. Dark phase adult rich uniform chestnut-brown, with grey tail. Pale phase adult brown above, buff below, with dark brown streaks and grey tail. Immature resembles duller version of adult of appropriate phase. Flight rapid and highly manoeuvrable among trees. Also hangs motionless on updraughts. Wings appear relatively slender and tail rather long. In flight, from below, black-outlined white underwings are characteristic of pale phase. Call a high-pitched, descending 'keeee'. Occurs in wooded valleys and hills, often with clearings. Nests in trees. Rather uncommon.

Short-toed Eagle *Circaetus gallicus* 65cm

This small, pale, buzzard-like eagle has a rather owl-like face. Adult and immature brown above, varying considerably. Head and breast show varying degrees of darker streaking and barring. Underparts characteristically appear near-white, with dark wingtips visible in flight. Head loose-feathered and appears bulky, almost owl-like. Tail long with faint darker bars. Often held fanned, especially when bird hovers with legs dangling – a diagnostic habit for a bird of this size in southern Europe. Call a harsh 'jeee' and barking 'ock-ock'. Occurs in well-wooded hillsides and gorges rich in snakes and lizards. Widespread in warmer areas but nowhere numerous.

43

Buzzard *Buteo buteo* 53cm

 A medium-sized, broad-winged bird of prey, the commonest of its size in the region. Adult and immature variable but normally darkish brown above and whitish below with heavy streaking. Occasional individuals may be buffish-white or almost all-dark. In flight, usually dark 'wrist' patches contrast with generally pale underwing. Soars well. Wings long and well-fingered, and tail relatively short and often fanned. Perches on telegraph poles or exposed branches. Call a far-carrying, cat-like mew. Occurs in open country, including farmland and moorland, with scattered clumps of trees for nesting. Widespread and locally common.

Honey Buzzard *Pernis apivorus* 52cm

 This buzzard-like bird of prey has a relatively long tail. Adult and immature normally dark brown above, but variable. Underparts white or buffish, streaked with brown. Head invariably grey, appearing disproportionately small, with yellow eye. Tail normally shows two dark bars near base and single broad bar near tip. In flight, wings relatively broad and fingered. Pale underwing has conspicuous dark 'wrist' patch, and striking, dark barring. Usual call a rapid 'kee-kee-kee'. Occurs in extensive areas of open forest, feeding on grubs of bees and wasps excavated from underground nests. Widespread but uncommon, except at favoured migration sites.

Red Kite *Milvus milvus* 62cm

This large bird of prey has a long, deeply forked tail. Adult has rufous-brown back. Head paler, often golden or almost white, with fine dark streaks. Breast and belly rufous, with dark brown streaks. Tail rich chestnut above, buffish-brown below with faint barring. Soars frequently, showing long, narrow-fingered wings, dark with large whitish patches at base of flight feathers. Immature resembles adult but duller with brownish head. In flight, wings held in characteristic 'M', tail constantly twisted. Utters buzzard-like mewing. Occurs in open woodland, often in hilly country. Widespread, rarely numerous. In Britain, confined to central Wales.

Goshawk *Accipiter gentilis* 55cm

A large, buzzard-sized hawk. Adult largely slate-grey above with brownish tinge. Crown and cheeks dark, separated by striking white eye-stripe extending on-to nape. Relatively long tail grey-brown with darker bars. Underparts white with fine, brown barring. Undertail white, with feathers fluffed out in display flights. Female appreciably larger than male. Immature brown above, buff below with darker streaks and buff eye-stripe. Silhouette with shortish, broad wings and long tail. Soars well; capable of fast, manoeuvrable flight in woodland. Call a chattering 'check'. Occurs in extensive areas of deciduous or coniferous forest. Widespread but nowhere numerous.

Sparrowhawk *Accipiter nisus* 35cm

A small, dashing hawk. Male dark grey above, grey crown and occasional white nape patch. Lacks eye-stripe. Tail long and grey, with several dark bars. Throat white; breast and belly white, closely barred with chestnut, appearing reddish at distance. Female appreciably larger than male, grey-brown above, white eye-stripe separates dark crown and cheeks. Underparts white, barred brown. Immature resembles female, but with brown streaks, not bars, on breast. Short, rounded wings and long tail, confer good speed and manoeuvrability. Call a rapid 'keck-keck-keck'. Occurs in all forest and woodland types. Widespread and often fairly common.

Marsh Harrier *Circus aeruginosus* 53cm

This medium-sized bird of prey has long, narrow wings and a long tail. Adult male largely brown above and chestnut below. Wings strikingly patterned, patches of brown and grey contrasting with black flight feathers. Tail pale grey. Adult female large, chocolate-brown with creamy-yellow on head. Immature predominantly brown with darker streaks, lacking yellow patches. Unlike most other harriers, neither sex has white rump. Characteristic flight low and steady, with frequent extended glides on wings held stiffly in shallow 'V'. Mostly silent. Occurs on marshland, usually with extensive reedbeds. Widespread. Locally common in southern Europe; scarce in Britain.

Hen Harrier *Circus cyaneus* 48cm

This medium-sized bird of prey has narrow wings and a long tail. Both sexes show white rump. Adult male has pale grey head, back and tail. Wings grey but flight feathers blackish. Female and immature rich brown with darker streaks. Tail brown with narrow dark bars. Female and immature very similar to slightly smaller, slimmer Montagu's Harrier. Feeds by quartering low over ground, powerful wingbeats interspersed with glides. In winter, sometimes roosts communally. Mostly silent. Occurs in open country. Breeds mainly on moorland and young conifer plantations. Winters on farmland, coastal or inland marshes and downland. Widespread but never numerous.

Montagu's Harrier *Circus pygargus* 40cm

A smallish, slim harrier which is elegant in flight. Adult male pale grey above, lacking white rump. Underparts greyish white, streaked chestnut on flanks. Wings grey above, with blackish flight feathers and dark bar near trailing edge. Female generally brown above and paler below with dark streaks. Immature similar but underparts richer rufous-brown. Female and immature show comparatively small white rump and long, black-barred, brown tail. Identified by narrow, pointed wings and buoyant flight. Call a shrill 'keck-keck-keck'. Occurs on open land including farmland and marshes. Widespread but only locally common. Scarce visitor to Britain.

Osprey *Pandion haliaetus* 58cm

A medium-sized, bird of prey which plunge-dives for fish. Adult and immature brown above, mostly white below, with often indistinct, brown breast band. Head white with large, brown patch through eye; crown loosely crested. Wings dark above, pale below, with dark wingtips and dark 'wrist' patch. In flight, wings held in characteristic arched 'M'. Beak grey and distinctly hooked. Legs and feet grey, with powerful talons. Mostly silent; sometimes brief whistle. Breeds beside northern lakes but coastal in south-west Europe. Widespread but never numerous. In Britain, breeds locally in Scotland. Migrants seen at wetlands outside breeding range.

Peregrine *Falco peregrinus* 45cm

A large, powerful falcon. Adult has steel-grey crown, back and tail. Dark moustachial stripes contrast with white cheeks. Underparts white, with delicate, brown-grey barring. Immature much browner with buffish breast heavily streaked with dark brown. Female appreciably larger than male. Flight fast and strong, typically with bursts of wingbeats interspersed with glides. Often hunts by 'stooping' - high-speed power dive of great force onto prey. Typical call a loud, chattering 'kek-kek-kek'. Occurs year-round in rocky, mountainous areas and on coastal cliffs. Also on moors and coastal marshes in winter. Widespread but nowhere numerous.

Hobby *Falco subbuteo* 28cm

This small, long-winged falcon has an elegant flight. Adult dark slate-grey above, conspicuously white on face and sides of neck (appearing as collar at distance), with black moustachial stripes. Underparts pale buff with heavy brownish streaking, shading to rich chestnut on lower flanks, thighs and undertail. Immature dull grey-brown above, heavily streaked buff below, lacking chestnut. Flight fast and aerobatic, resembling giant Swift; catches birds, bats and insects. Call an insistent, chattering 'ki-ki-ki'. Breeds on heaths and in open woodland with adjacent farmland or marshes. Widespread and locally fairly common visitor from May to August.

Merlin *Falco columbarius* 30cm

A small, low-flying falcon. Adult male slate-grey above and rich chestnut-buff below with dark brown streaks. Moustachial stripes indistinct. Female and immature dark brown above and buff below, streaked with dark brown. Flight fast and agile, hunting small birds in low-level chases across open country. Also seen perched on isolated posts and circling high above. Call a chattering 'ki-ki-ki'. Breeds on moorland and grassy uplands. Winters over farmland and inland and coastal marshes. Widespread but rather scarce. In Britain, scarce breeding species, mainly in north and west, but winters around coasts throughout.

Kestrel *Falco tinnunculus* 35cm

This very familiar, hawk-like falcon is the commonest and most widespread of its size in Europe. The adult male has chestnut-brown upperparts with dark brown spots and buffish underparts, also with dark spots. Head grey and tail grey with black terminal bar. Female and immature brown above and buff below with heavy, brown spots and

female (above)
male and female at nest (below)

streaks. Long, pointed wings sometimes appear rather rounded. Distinctive in flight. Hovers frequently and expertly, often on motorway verges. Call a shrill and repetitive 'ki-ki-ki'. Found in a wide variety of habitats, from towns and cities to farmland, marshes, moors and sea cliffs. Widespread and common throughout.

Red Grouse *Lagopus lagopus scoticus* 40cm

This medium-sized gamebird is a subspecies of the Willow Grouse of mainland Europe. Adult male rich chestnut-brown with dark wings. Female similar but less rufous. Plumage is retained all through year. Remains concealed among heather until startled. Then flies low over moors, long glides on bowed wings with bouts of rapid wingbeats. Typical call 'go-back go-back go-back'. Occurs on heather moors with willow, birch and juniper scrub, in northern England, Scotland and Wales. Similar but separate subspecies in Ireland. WILLOW GROUSE (*Lagopus lagopus*) occurs from Scandinavia eastwards. Similar to Red Grouse in summer but has white wings. In winter, acquires all-white plumage.

Ptarmigan *Lagopus mutus* 35cm

This medium-sized gamebird is exclusive to uplands. Summer adult male has head, neck and back mottled greyish-brown, with black tail. Breast and belly white, white wings conspicuous in flight. Red, fleshy wattle over eye visible at close range. Summer adult female largely mottled chestnut-brown, with white wings. Immature similar. In winter, both sexes all-white with black tail and small black eye-patch in male. Usually runs rather than flies. Calls include various croaks. Male has brief, crowing 'song'. Occurs year-round at high altitudes or high latitudes, associated with mosses and lichens. Widespread in Europe within habitat.

Black Grouse *Tetrao tetrix* 50cm

A large, robust gamebird. Male unmistakable with glossy black plumage and black and white lyre-shaped tail. Shows large red wattles over eyes and, in flight, white 'shoulder' and wingbar conspicuous on blackish, rounded wings. Female and immature mottled grey-brown, with relatively long, slightly forked tail. Displays communally at lekking grounds, mostly around dawn. When disturbed, flight is high and fast. At leks, utters astonishing variety of cackling, bubbling and crooning calls. Occurs on heaths and moors, especially adjacent to areas of woodland or conifer plantations. Also in open woodland. Widespread but only locally common.

Capercaillie *Tetrao urogallus* 85cm

A huge, turkey-like gamebird. Adult male unmistakable. Mainly glossy black but back brownish. Head feathers form shaggy crest and has red wattles over eyes. Displays with long tail fanned. Female and immature smaller (but still large for gamebirds), richly marked chestnut-brown. Despite size can be remarkably elusive. Both sexes have disyllabic 'kok-kok' call. Male song accelerating series of 'hiccups', ending in 'pop', recalling cork being withdrawn from bottle. Occurs in coniferous woodland. Widespread but seldom common. In Britain, re-established in pinewoods of central Scotland having formerly become extinct.

Red-legged Partridge *Alectoris rufa* 35cm

This medium-sized gamebird has characteristic red legs and bill. Adult grey-brown above and buffish below, the flanks with bold barring of black, white and chestnut. Striking head pattern of white chin and upper throat, surrounded by black border and black streaking extending onto breast. Immature sandy brown, lacking head pattern. Prefers to run from danger but if disturbed, flies low and direct on whirring wings. Sometimes perches on fence posts. Call a loud 'chuck, chuck-arr'. Found on dry arable fields, heaths and areas of scrub. Locally common, numbers and range strongly influenced by release of birds for hunting.

Grey Partridge *Perdix perdix* 30cm

A medium-sized gamebird. Adult has buff-streaked brownish face, upper throat and back. Nape and breast dove-grey, paling towards belly. Bold chestnut barring on flanks. Dark brown, inverted horseshoe patch on belly, larger in male than female. Immature streaked sandy brown. Flight low, direct and fast, on whirring wings. Call a distinct 'chirrick, chirrick'. Occurs in arable fields, grassland, heaths and scrub. Widespread and locally common. QUAIL (*Coturnix coturnix*) is superficially similar but much smaller. Seldom seen, but characteristic 'wet-my-lips' call is a familiar sound in meadows and grasslands of southern Europe.

Pheasant *Phasianus colchicus* 85cm

male (left) and female (right)

A large, beautifully marked, very long-tailed game-bird. Adult unmistakable with shiny, orange-brown body. Head and neck glossy, bottle-green, with scarlet face patches. Neck and body separated by white collar in some birds. Female and immature sandy buff with darker streaks, and shorter tail. Prefers to run from danger but, if alarmed, take-off explosive and noisy. Flight of limited duration, rapid with long glides after bursts of flapping. Male utters ringing 'cork-cork', followed by loud wing-claps. Occurs in farmland, parkland, shrubberies, reeds, scrub and open woodland. Widespread. Numbers and distribution influenced by release of reared birds for hunting.

Crane *Grus grus* 110cm

A huge, stork-like bird. Adult predominantly greyish. Long neck black in front, white behind, extending up to eye. Small red crown patch extends as black down nape. Bushy plumes above tail give bottom-heavy appearance, especially in spring. Beak grey, long and dagger-like. Legs long and grey. Immature grey-brown, paler below. Extremely wary. Flies on broad, fingered wings with neck and legs outstretched, flocks often in 'V'-formation. Loud trumpeting calls in flight; wild, whooping calls during display. Breeds on extensive northern bogs and tundra. Winters at traditional areas in western Europe. Regular on established migration routes.

Great Bustard *Otis tarda* 100cm

This is one of the heaviest flying birds in Europe. Adult male heavily barred, golden brown above and white below. Long neck and head grey, with white moustachial tufts. Bill yellowish, short and stout. Legs yellowish, stout and long. Female and immature drabber, less finely marked, lacks moustachial tufts. Flies with neck and legs outstretched, with striking black and white broad wings. Very wary. Mostly silent. Occurs on stony plains and large, open fields of grain and other crops. Rare and local. Small flocks move west in severe winter weather. LITTLE BUSTARD (*Tetrax tetrax*) much smaller, male with black neck in summer. Locally common in southern Europe but difficult to see.

Water Rail *Rallus aquaticus* 28cm

A medium-sized, skulking waterbird. Adult predominantly leaden grey on face and underparts, with flanks boldly barred black and white. Undertail coverts strikingly white. Upperparts rich buffish-brown, speckled and streaked with dark brown. Beak reddish, long, slender and slightly downcurved. Legs and long toes pinkish-brown. Immature darker, more speckled above and barred below. Flies rarely, fluttering low with legs trailing. Utters various noisy, pig-like grunts and squeals. Occurs in dense reedbeds and heavily vegetated swamps; sometimes in streams and ditches in winter. Widespread but seldom numerous. More often heard than seen.

Corncrake *Crex crex* 23cm

A skulking, medium-sized crake, which is more often heard than seen. Adult predominantly richly mottled buffish-brown above, with strikingly chestnut wings. Throat grey but rest of underparts buff, barred with brown on flanks. Feeble flight shows chestnut wings, with brownish legs trailing. Beak pinkish with darker tip. Immature resembles paler, washed-out version of adult. Call is absolutely diagnostic: dry 'crex-crex', repeated endlessly day and night. Occurs from April to August in hay meadows and unkempt grassland. Widespread and locally common in mainland Europe. Scarce and declining in Britain, and virtually confined to Western Isles of Scotland.

Moorhen *Gallinula chloropus* 33cm

A medium-sized waterbird, the adult has mostly velvety brownish-black plumage. Shows characteristic white streak along flanks and white under-tail coverts, particularly conspicuous when tail jerked while swimming. Forehead scarlet and fleshy, beak red with yellow tip. Legs and long toes greenish-yellow. Immature drab grey-brown, darker above than below. Swims well. Upends to feed, but does not dive. Flies feebly and low over water with legs trailing. Generally rather nervous but becomes confiding in many urban settings. Utters several ringing calls, including 'whittuck'. Occurs on wide variety of fresh waters, from small ponds to large lakes. Common.

Coot *Fulica atra* 38cm

A medium-sized waterbird, the adult has uniformly dull, velvety black plumage. Short bill and fleshy forehead patch diagnostically white. Legs and feet grey, the toes with distinct lobed webbing. Immature dark grey-brown above and paler below. Flies low over water, revealing conspicuous white trailing edges to wings. Swims buoyantly and dives frequently to feed on water plants. Call a single or repeated, strident 'kowk'. Occurs on larger expanses of fresh or brackish water. In winter, often occurs on reservoirs, sometimes in large flocks. Occasionally also on sheltered estuaries. Common and widespread throughout the region.

Oystercatcher *Haematopus ostralegus* 43cm

A conspicuously pied, medium-sized wader. Adult has black back, head and neck with white underparts. Tail white with black terminal band. Stout bill orange-red; legs and feet pink, thick and fleshy. Winter adult and immature show some black on beak and white collar mark on neck. Usually flies in noisy flocks, black wings show conspicuous white wingbars. Alert, responding noisily to intruders. Calls include various shrill pipings. Breeds on shingle and sandy beaches, other coastal habitats, occasionally inland. Feeds and winters on rocky, sandy or muddy coasts and estuaries. Widespread and often common. In winter, usually seen in flocks.

Lapwing *Vanellus vanellus* 30cm

An unmistakable medium-sized plover. Adult is black above with purplish-green, iridescent sheen. Cheeks greyish but throat, breast and crown black. Conspicuous, long, slender, upturned crest. Flanks and belly white. Undertail coverts rich chestnut and tail white with terminal black bar. Bill black and rather stubby, legs long and reddish-brown. Immature browner, with buff fringes to feathers, giving scaly appearance to back. In flight, has floppy wingbeats on black and white, rounded wings. Call a characteristic 'pe-wit'. Breeds on fields, moors and marshes. Winters on arable land, grassland and estuaries. Common.

57

Ringed Plover *Charadrius hiaticula* 20cm

A small, active plover. Adult sandy brown above and white below, with black collar. Head has black and white facial pattern, lacking upper white forehead stripe and yellow eye-ring of Little Ringed Plover. Stubby bill is orange with black tip. Legs orange-yellow. White wingbar conspicuous in flight. Immature has black markings replaced by brown. Feeds characteristically by running rapidly, then pausing motionless before bending to pick up food. Rarely seen in large flocks. Call a fluting 'too-lee' and song trilling. Occurs on sandy coasts, estuaries and saltpans, very occasionally inland on river banks. Widespread and relatively common.

Little Ringed Plover *Charadrius dubius* 15cm

This active wader is smaller than Ringed Plover but with similar breast markings. Adult pale sandy brown above and white below. Bold black and white head pattern, with white band between black forehead and sandy crown. Has black collar band and yellow eye-ring. Dark bill has yellowish base. Legs pale yellowish. Immature lacks black and white pattern, has brownish, incomplete collar. In flight, shows plain, pale brown wings, with little trace of wingbar. Usually singly or in pairs. Call a plaintive, piping 'tee-you'; trilling song. Breeds on sandy or gravel shores of rivers or inland lakes. In Britain, prefers gravel pits. Seen on coast on migration. Widespread.

Kentish Plover *Charadrius alexandrinus* 15cm

A small, active plover with an incomplete dark collar and dark legs. Adult pale, sandy brown above and white below. Male has chestnut crown, black and white forehead pattern, black stripe through eye and dark patches on shoulders. Female and immature lack chestnut crown and black markings replaced by brown. Bill is all-dark. In flight, white wingbar visible in brown wings. Calls include a fluting 'poo-eet' and a soft, repeated 'wit'. This distinguishes it from Ringed Plover. Trilling song. Nests on sandy beaches, saltpans and margins of muddy lagoons. Locally common in southern Europe. Despite English name, a rare visitor to Britain.

Dotterel *Charadrius morinellus* 22cm

A medium-sized, plump-looking upland plover. Summer adult grey-brown above with black crown and distinctive, bold white eye-stripe. Throat white, breast and nape grey. Belly chestnut, darker on flanks, separated from breast by clear, narrow white band. Undertail white, bill dark and stubby. Legs yellow. Female brighter than male, who incubates eggs. Winter adult and immature buff above, paler below, with suggestion of eye-stripe and breast band patterning of adult. No wingbar visible in flight. Confiding. Call a soft, piping trill. Breeds on tundra and plateaux mountain tops. Seen on airfields and grassy fields on migration. Scarce.

Grey Plover *Pluvialis squatarola* 28cm

A medium-sized, often solitary plover. Summer adult strikingly handsome with upperparts richly black-flecked silver grey, separated from black face, throat, breast and belly by broad, white margin. In Europe, winter adult or immature mostly seen, with flecked grey-buff upperparts and white underparts. In flight, shows faint wingbar and diagnostic bold black 'armpits' beneath wings. Stubby beak and legs black. Call a plaintive, fluting 'tee-loo-ee', recalling a human wolf-whistle. Breeds on northern tundra. Winters on sheltered coasts and estuaries. Widespread but rarely numerous from September to April. Newly returned migrants often still in summer plumage.

Golden Plover *Pluvialis apricaria* 28cm

This medium-sized, attractive plover has a rather rotund body, round head, short bill and long legs. Similar to Grey Plover but less bulky. Summer adult striking, with richly flecked, golden crown, nape and back separated from glossy black face, throat and belly by broad, white margin. Stubby beak and legs greyish. Winter adult and immature flecked dull golden buff above and buff below, shading to white on belly. In flight, shows no wingbar, has white 'armpits' beneath wings. Gregarious outside breeding season. Call a fluting whistle 'tloo-ee'. Breeds on tundra and moorland. Winters on damp fields and grassland, often near coasts but also well inland. Locally common. This species sometimes appears in large flocks in winter, and is often associated with Lapwings.

60

Woodcock *Scolopax rusticola* 35cm

This medium-sized, dumpy, woodland wader has a very long bill. Adult and immature superficially Snipe-like, but more heavily built, with bolder barring and finer mottling on rich brown plumage. Breast grey-buff and barred, not streaked. Head angular with large bulging eyes and crosswise yellowish bands on rich brown crown. Beak pinkish-brown, long and stout. Rarely flies until danger is close. During winter and spring displays, establishes regular 'roding' flight paths through woodland glades. During display, utters frog-like 'orrrt-orrrt', with repeated, high-pitched 'swick' calls. Found year-round in damp woodland. Widespread but difficult to see.

Common Snipe *Gallinago gallinago* 28cm

A smallish wader with a very long, straight bill. Adult and immature rich brown, heavily barred and streaked with chestnut, buff and black. Three, bold, yellowish-buff, longitudinal stripes on crown. Beak brownish, legs greenish and comparatively short. Swift, zig-zag flight when flushed; wingbars and striped back conspicuous, tail rounded with dark band. During display flight, dives with tail fanned, producing bleating noise. Feeds by probing vertically with bill. On taking flight, utters harsh 'scarp'. When breeding, utters clock-like 'ticker, tick-er'. Breeds on freshwater marshes, wet meadows and moors. Winters similarly, but also on coastal marshes.

61

Curlew *Numenius arquata* 58cm

 A large, unmistakable wader with an exceptionally long, downcurved bill. Adult and immature sandy-buff above, with whitish and brown flecks and streaks. Underparts pale buffish-fawn with darker brown streaks and spots, shading to white on belly. Bill brownish-black. Legs blue-grey and relatively long. In flight, shows clear white rump extending up back, and dark-barred buff tail. No distinctive wingbars. Often gregarious in winter. Call a characteristic 'coor-lee'. When breeding, performs song flight combining calls with remarkable bubbling trills. Breeds on moorland, marshes and wet meadows. Winters on coasts and estuaries. Widespread and often common.

Whimbrel *Numenius phaeopus* 40cm

 A large wader, similar to Curlew, but smaller. Adult and immature greyish-brown above, with copious white and dark brown flecking. Underparts pale buff with dark brown streaking, shading to white on belly. Crown dark brown, with three, yellow-buff, longitudinal stripes. Beak grey-brown, long (not as dramatically as Curlew) and downcurved. Legs blue-grey. In flight, shows uniform wings, only small whitish rump patch and buff tail with darker bars. Mostly solitary. Call a series of high-pitched whistles, often repeated seven times. Breeds on moors and tundra. Usually migrates on estuaries and coasts. Widespread but seldom numerous.

Black-tailed Godwit *Limosa limosa* 40cm

This large wader has a long, straight bill. Summer adult striking, back mottled brown with chestnut and whitish underparts and chestnut barring on flanks. Head and neck cinnamon-brown. Winter adult and immature grey or grey-brown above, paling to near-white below. In flight, always shows striking, broad, white bar in blackish wings and black-tipped white tail. Beak pinkish with blackish tip. Legs long and black. Gregarious outside breeding season. Call a noisy 'wicka-wicka-wicka', particularly when breeding. Breeds on damp meadows and marshes. Winters on estuaries. Locally common.

Bar-tailed Godwit *Limosa lapponica* 40cm

A rather large wader with a long, straight bill. Summer adult has richly marked brown back and chestnut belly. Head, neck and breast rufous cinnamon-brown. Winter adult and immature mottled grey to grey-brown above, shading to white below. In flight, shows no wingbars. Narrow, brown barring across white tail best seen in flight. Beak reddish but darker towards tip, very long and slightly, but noticeably, upturned. Legs long and black. Gregarious outside breeding season; sometimes in large flocks. Breeds on Arctic tundra; winters on muddy or sandy estuaries and sheltered, coastal bays. Common and locally numerous.

63

Turnstone *Arenaria interpres* 23cm

 This small, dumpy wader has a short, chisel-like bill, used for turning over stones and seaweed. Summer adult has richly marked pale chestnut back, white head, neck and underparts, and whole body patterned with black. In western Europe, winter and immature more usually seen, where pied parts of plumage retained but chestnut replaced with grey. Feeds among seaweeds on rocky shores where extremely well camouflaged. Legs orange. Call a staccato, chattering 'tuk-tuk-tuk'. Breeds on tundra and rocky Arctic coasts. Winters on rocky coasts, occasionally also on estuaries. Widespread and often common in suitable habitats.

Common Sandpiper *Actitis hypoleucos* 20cm

 This small wader has a distinctive flight and an incessantly bobbing gait. Summer adult sandy-brown above, flecked with white. Underparts white with brown streaking on throat; sides of breast form half collar. Winter adult and immature duller, less strongly marked. Bill short, straight and pinkish with dark tip. Legs yellowish-green. Flight low over water and fast, with rapid shallow wingbeats on downcurved wings. In flight, shows white wingbar, brown rump and brown tail with brown-barred white outer feathers. Call a trilling 'twee-wee-wee'. Song 'tittyweety-tittyweety'. Breeds beside lakes and rivers. Invariably migrates by fresh water. Widespread.

Green Sandpiper *Tringa ochropus* 23cm

This small wader appears dark above and light below. Adult and immature dark greenish-grey crown, nape and back, faintly speckled with whitish buff, more marked in summer adult. Underparts white, dark streaks on breast. Beak dark, medium length. Legs yellowish-green. Flight jerky and Snipe-like, dark wings contrast with white rump. White tail has strong, black barring. Underwings blackish. Often bobs. Usually solitary. Call 'tee-loo-eet'; fluty, trilling song. Breeds close to water in swampy forests, may use old nests in trees. On migration and in winter, frequents inland pools, streams and watercress beds. Regular but never numerous.

Wood Sandpiper *Tringa glareola* 20cm

A small, elegantly proportioned wader. Summer adult brownish above, copiously flecked with white. White underparts have light flecking and streaking on neck and sides of breast. Clear, pale, buff-white eye-stripe below dark cap. Winter adult and immature duller, grey-brown. Beak dark, shortish and straight. Legs yellow and relatively long. In flight, shows whitish underwings, white rump and tail with faint dark barring. No wingbars. Mostly solitary. Call a distinct 'chiff-if-if'. Musical, yodelling song flight. Breeds on swampy moorland and tundra, often with scattered trees. Migrates on marshes and pools. Widespread and regular but seldom numerous.

Redshank *Tringa totanus* 28cm

This medium-sized wader has bright red legs. Summer adult rich brown above with pale flecks and fine dark brown streaks. Underparts buff with brown streaking, shading to white on belly. Winter adult and immature duller grey-brown above. Underparts grey-buff, shading to white on belly and flanks. Bill reddish, slim and medium length. Legs red throughout year. Bold white wingbar distinctive in flight. Wary and noisy. Piping calls include variants of 'tu-lee-lee'. Breeds on marshland, wet meadows and moorland. Winters on estuaries, sandy bays and freshwater marshes. Widespread and common, especially on coasts.

Greenshank *Tringa nebularia* 30cm

A medium-sized, elegant wader with a long, slightly upturned bill. Summer adult grey-brown above, richly flecked with black and silver, white below. Winter adult and immature paler and drabber grey, may appear very white. Bill greenish; legs greenish-yellow, long and relatively stout. In flight, shows all-dark wings with no wingbars, striking white rump extends well up back. Tail white. Mostly solitary. Call a far-carrying, tri-syllabic 'tu-tu-tu'. Breeds on damp moorland, marshes and tundra. Migrates and winters on coastal lagoons and sheltered sandy or muddy estuaries. Occasionally on freshwater pools. Widespread but seldom numerous.

Ruff *Philomachus pugnax* 30cm

A medium-sized wader. Breeding adult male unmistakable, ruff of feathers round neck usually chestnut, black or white. Back mottled rich brown and underparts mostly white. Appreciably smaller female mottled buff and brown above, paler buff below. Winter male and immature similar to female. Bill yellowish-red with dark tip. Legs usually orange. In flight, appears long-winged with pale wingbar. Tail with dark central bar separating white oval patches on each side of rump. Gregarious. Forms communal leks in breeding season. Mostly silent. Breeds on marshes, wet fields and tundra. Otherwise on coastal lagoons and inland pools. Seldom numerous.

Knot *Calidris canutus* 25cm

A medium-small wader. Summer adult reddish-brown above, with golden, scaly markings, and distinctly rusty below. Winter adult and immature lack any distinctive features. Grey-brown upperparts and whitish below. Immature has buffish flush and rather scaly appearance to upperparts due to pale feather margins. Bill medium length, dark and straight; legs dull yellowish. Faint white wingbar visible in flight. Gregarious outside breeding season, gathering in close-packed flocks, thousands strong. Call a soft 'knut'. Breeds on Arctic tundra; winters on sand and mudflats of estuaries. Widespread and locally numerous from September to April.

Purple Sandpiper *Calidris maritima* 20cm

A small, rather dumpy wader, characteristic of rocky shores. Summer adult has rich brown back with buff, scaly markings. Underparts almost entirely white, browner on flanks. Winter adult and immature distinctive purplish-leaden grey on upperparts and breast, but paler grey below with white throat. Pale yellowish eye-ring. Slightly downcurved bill is yellow with black tip; legs yellow. In flight, shows indistinct wingbar but some white on inner flight feathers. Dark tail has white patches on each side of rump. Call a disyllabic 'wit-wit'. Breeds on moorland and tundra. Otherwise, invariably on .seaweed-clad rocky shores. Locally common.

Sanderling *Calidris alba* 20cm

A small, fast-running wader, typical of sandy beaches. Summer adult rufous cinnamon above with scaly, buff markings, and white below. In Europe, winter adult or immature more usually seen, with upperparts pale silver-grey and pure white underparts. Shows grey-black smudge through eye and black 'shoulder' patch often visible. Bill dark and short and legs black. In flight, white wingbar conspicuous on dark wings. Runs as if powered by clockwork along sandy beaches, typically following waves in and out. Breeds on Arctic tundra. On passage and in winter, found on sandy beaches. Locally common from September to April.

Dunlin *Calidris alpina* 18cm

This small, long-billed wader is the commonest of its size in the region. Summer adult has upperparts rich brown with darker feathering, underparts pale with black belly patch. Winter adult and immature upperparts grey-brown, with variable amounts of grey, black and brown feathering in autumn. Underparts white but immature has black spots on flanks. Bill dark, downcurved, variable in length. Legs dark. In flight, shows pale wingbar and white sides to dark tail. Gregarious outside breeding season, often in huge flocks. Call a nasal 'treeer'. Trilling song in flight. Breeds on wetlands, moors and tundra. Otherwise, mainly on estuaries.

Curlew Sandpiper *Calidris ferruginea* 20cm

This smallish wader has a noticeably downcurved bill. Summer adult chestnut-brown, with duller, brown wings. Winter adult and immature paler with grey-brown upperparts, buffish-white underparts and clear, white eye-stripe. Immature in autumn has scaly back due to pale feather margins. Beak dark and long. Legs dark and relatively long. In flight, shows pale wingbar and prominent white rump, contrasting with black tail. Often in small flocks. Call a soft, trilling 'chirrup'. Breeds on tundra. Otherwise, occurs on estuaries, saline lagoons and marshes. In Europe, seen mainly on migration. Regular, numbers varying from year to year.

Little Stint *Calidris minuta* 13cm

This tiny, short-billed wader is a rather shorter version of a Dunlin. Summer adult has brown and buff upperparts, with dark centres to feathers on back. Pale buff V-marking on back, white underparts. Winter adult grey-brown above and white below. Immature upperparts rufous and black, pale V-mark on back and pale stripe over eye. Bill and legs dark in all stages. In flight, shows pale wingbar and tail with dark centre and grey outer feathers. Call a terse 'chit'. Breeds on tundra. Migrates on muddy pools, saline lagoons and marshes. In western Europe, juvenile mainly seen, on migration in autumn. Widespread but seldom common. TEMMINCK'S STINT (*Calidris temminckii*) is marginally smaller and much more grey and uniformly marked.

Avocet *Recurvirostra avosetta* 43cm

This medium-sized wader, has unmistakable pied plumage and a long, upturned bill. Adult predominantly white, with black crown and nape, black bars on back and wings and black wingtips. Beak black, slender and upturned. Feeds by sweeping bill from side-to-side in shallow water. Legs blue-grey and long. Immature similar but black in plumage replaced by brownish feathering. Vocal, uttering 'kloo-oot' call, varying from flute-like to strident if alarmed. Found on saline or brackish lagoons and pools, breeding colonially. Some overwinter on estuaries, forming small flocks. Locally common, especially in southern Europe.

Black-winged Stilt *Himantopus himantopus* 38cm

This quite unmistakable medium-sized wader has incredibly long legs and pied plumage. Adult has black back and wings, white head, neck and underparts, and varying amounts of grey or black on nape and face. Beak black, long and slender. Legs rich pink, their length enabling it to feed in deeper water than other waders. Immature browner above with greyish-pink legs. In flight, wings reveal dark undersides and no wingbars, and legs trail conspicuously beyond tail. Noisily vocal, uttering yelping 'kyip' call. Occurs on saltpans, coastal lagoons and marshes. Locally common in southern Europe, rare in the north-west.

Stone Curlew *Burhinus oedicnemus* 40cm

This medium-sized, thick-set and slow-moving wader is most ungainly. Mostly sandy-buff, paling to white on belly. Head, neck and back finely marked with dark brown streaks. Dark stripe through large, glaring yellow eye, with pale buff stripes above and below. Plover-like bill is yellow with black tip. Legs long and yellow, with large, knobbly joints. Double white wingbars and white wing patches show in swift, direct flight. Secretive and retiring, most active after dark. Utters weird, wailing calls and shrieks, some reminiscent of Oystercatcher or Curlew. Breeds on stony, sandy and chalky ground, dry heaths and arable fields. Scarce and easily overlooked.

Pratincole *Glareola pratincola* 25cm

A smallish, atypical wader. In silhouette, on the ground and in flight, resembles large Swallow or even a tern. Adult mostly sandy-brown above, paling to white on belly. Characteristic buff throat patch edged in black. Beak dark with red base. Legs black and short. Immature has more scaly appearance to upperparts and indistinct throat patch. Flight Swallow-like, showing black wingtips, reddish-chestnut underwing, white rump and deeply forked, black tail. Calls include various chatterings and a tern-like 'keeyik'. Breeds colonially on coastal mudflats and saltpans. Locally common in southern Europe and rare vagrant further north.

Grey Phalarope *Phalaropus fulicarius* 17cm

A small, dumpy, highly aquatic wader. Summer adult has orange-red throat, breast and flanks, paling to white on belly. Back brown with pale markings and head has white cheek patch. Female brighter than male. Bill yellowish. Winter adult has grey upperparts, white underparts and black 'panda' patch through eye. Bill dark. Immature like winter adult but with mottled back. In flight, shows single white wingbar. Invariably seen swimming buoyantly, sometimes spinning. Call a sharp 'whit'. Breeds beside tundra pools, from Iceland northwards. Winters far out to sea. Occasionally on coasts after severe autumn gales in winter or immature plumages.

Red-necked Phalarope *Phalaropus lobatus* 17cm

This small, slim, wader spends most of its time in the water. Summer adult has mottled brown and buff upperparts and dark head. Throat and chin white, reddish stripe on side of slim neck. Underparts white. Female brighter than male. Winter adult has grey upperparts, white head and neck, dark smudge through eye, and white underparts. Immature similar but upperparts with brown feathering. Dark, finely pointed bill. In flight, shows double white wingbar and black tail with grey outer feathers. Swims buoyantly, often spinning. Call a sharp 'prip'. Breeds beside moorland or tundra pools. Winters at sea. On inshore waters, mainly during severe autumn gales. Rather scarce.

Great Skua *Stercorarius skua* 60cm

A superficially gull-like seabird but bulky and heavily built, with a powerful, direct flight. It is the largest but least agile of the skuas. Adult dark brown, with paler and darker flecking. Cheeks slightly paler and crown slighter darker. In flight, bold white flashes on dark wings distinguish it from immature large gulls. Pursues other birds up to Gannet-size to pirate food. Utters a barking 'tuk' or 'uk-uk-uk', and a rasping 'skeeer'. Breeds on moorland, tundra and remote islands. Winters out at sea but may pass through coastal waters on migration. Locally numerous at breeding colonies but scarce on migration in spring and autumn.

Arctic Skua *Stercorarius parasiticus* 45cm

A graceful, gull-like seabird with two colour forms. Dark phase adult uniformly chocolate brown. Pale phase adult sandy-brown above, with dark cap and buffish-white neck, breast and belly. Adult tail has central feathers elongated and pointed. Immature rich brown, heavily speckled and barred, lacks long central tail feathers. Beak and legs greyish-brown. In flight, all show white patches on wings. Pursues other birds to steal food. Calls include yelping 'tuk-tuk'. Breeds in loose colonies on moorland, tundra and remote islands. May migrate in inshore waters. Locally fairly common at breeding colonies but is otherwise rather scarce.

Great Black-backed Gull *Larus marinus* 68cm

The largest European gull. Adult largely white, with black back and wings. In flight, wings show white trailing edge and white spots near tips. Bill yellow with red spot near tip, large and powerful. Legs pink. Immature speckled brown and white tail with broad, black terminal bar. Takes four years to reach adult plumage. Flight powerful and heavy. Utters a gruff 'kow-kow-kow'. Pairs nest in isolation on islands and coastal cliffs. Feeds on carrion, takes young of smaller seabirds. Most maritime of the large gulls. Winters along coasts, also inland, especially near refuse tips. Widespread and fairly common.

Lesser Black-backed Gull *Larus fuscus* 53cm

This medium-sized gull is noticeably smaller than superficially similar Great Black-backed Gull. Adult predominantly white with slate-grey back and wings. Wingtips black with small white markings. Bill yellow, with red spot near tip, and legs bright yellow. Immature mottled brown and white above, and pale below. Often almost indistinguishable from immature Herring Gull. Gregarious, nesting in colonies. Utters loud 'key-ow' and various laughing and mewing calls. Breeds on cliffs, islands and sand-dunes. Migrates south in winter to coastal and inland habitats including reservoirs and refuse tips. Widespread and locally common.

Herring Gull *Larus argentatus* 55cm

A medium-sized gull. Adult predominantly white with silver-grey back and wings. Wingtips black, with bold white markings. Bill yellow, with red spot near tip. Legs pink. Immature mottled brown and white above and largely white below; bill and legs brownish. Gregarious. Vocal, uttering mewing cries and various laughing calls. Breeds on cliffs, remote islands, sand-dunes and buildings. Winters on coasts, farmland, reservoirs and refuse tips. Common and often numerous in north-west Europe. Replaced in Mediterranean by closely related and similar YELLOW-LEGGED GULL (*Larus cachinnans*), with yellow, not pink, legs.

Glaucous Gull *Larus hyperboreus* 67cm

A large, very pale gull. Adult predominantly white with pale grey wings, entirely lacking black tips. Bill yellow with red spot near tip, large and powerful. Orange eye-ring, visible at close range. Legs pink. Immature mottled, pale coffee brown, becoming almost pure white, including wings, in second year. At rest, folded wings barely reach tip of tail. Great Black-backed Gull profile and size distinguish from similar but smaller ICELAND GULL (*Larus glaucoides*). Voice similar to Herring Gull. Breeds colonially on cliffs and islands in Arctic. Winters around coasts further south. Occasionally seen inland, especially at refuse tips. Scarce.

Common Gull *Larus canus* 40cm

A medium-sized gull. Adult predominantly white, with grey flecks around head and nape in winter. Wings grey above with black and white tips to flight feathers. Bill yellow and unmarked, legs greenish-yellow and eye dark. Immature pale brown above and whitish below. Crown and nape streaked grey-brown and bill pink with dark tip. Rather gregarious. Utters high-pitched 'kee-you' and high 'gah-gah-gah' calls. Breeds on remote hillsides, islands, moors and tundra. Widespread on migration and in winter, on farmland, urban parks, refuse tips, reservoirs and coasts. Locally common, especially in the north of the range.

Kittiwake *Rissa tridactyla* 40cm

This medium-sized, slim-winged gull is a truly marine species. Adult mostly white with pale grey upperwings. Tips of flight feathers black, with no white patches. Bill lemon yellow with vermilion gape visible at close range. Legs short and black. Immature has blackish collar, black 'M' markings across wings, and black-tipped, shallowly forked tail visible in flight. In all stages, wings characteristically long and slender. Flight buoyant. Vocal at colonies, uttering distinctive 'kitt-week' calls. Nests colonially on sea cliffs, occasionally on coastal buildings. Otherwise, occurs mostly far out to sea. Widespread and locally common.

Mediterranean Gull *Larus melanocephala* 38cm

A medium-sized gull. Summer adult largely white, with black hood. Upperwing pale grey, tips white with no black markings. Relatively large bill orange-red, black band near tip. Legs reddish-brown. Winter adult lacks dark head, dark smudge through eye appears menacing. Immature has brown inner forewing and black outer wing. In flight, shows broad, black terminal bar on white tail. Typical call 'cow-cow-cow'. Breeds on wetlands and coastal marshes. Winters along coasts, scarce inland. Locally common at colonies in south-east Europe, otherwise scarce. In north-west Europe, mainly winter visitor, may breed among Black-headed Gulls.

Black-headed Gull *Larus ridibundus* 35cm

summer (above)
winter (below)

A familiar gull of a medium-size. Summer adult is white, with chocolate hood. Upperwings pale silver grey, with black-tipped white flight feathers. White leading edge to wing diagnostic in flight. Bill and legs blood red. Winter adult loses brown hood but has dark feathering on nape and smudge through eye. Bill and legs are duller. Immature has brownish bars on inner portion of wing and black terminal band on white tail, best seen in flight. Gregarious. Breeds colonially on dunes, islands and coastal and freshwater marshes. In winter, is almost ubiquitous on the coast and inland, including urban areas but excluding mountains. Common and often abundant.

Little Gull *Larus minutus* 27cm

The smallest, regularly seen gull in the region. Summer adult largely white, with black-hood. Wings grey above with white wingtips and trailing edge, but diagnostically sooty-grey below. Bill small and dark and legs red. Winter adult lacks black head. Immature has white underwing, slightly forked black-tipped tail, and black 'M'-marking across upperwing. Swims buoyantly. Flight distinctive and tern-like. Utters high-pitched 'kek-kek-kek'. Breeds on freshwater marshes. Winters mainly at sea, sometimes coastally. In north-west Europe, mainly seen on migration when occasionally occurs inland. Locally common at colonies but elsewhere rather scarce.

Black Tern *Chlidonias niger* 25cm

This small, dark tern has a graceful flight. Summer adult largely sooty-grey with jet black head, breast and belly. Tail dark grey and shallowly forked. Bill and legs dark. Winter adult grey above, white below, with dark crown, white forehead and black 'half-collar' marks on shoulders. Immature similar to winter adult but browner. Characteristic flight, dipping down to water surface to feed. Gregarious where common. Mostly silent. Breeds colonially on swamps and marshes. In north-west Europe, seen most frequently on migration, in May and September. Sometimes lingers at coastal marshes and inland wetlands. Regular and locally common.

Little Tern *Sterna albifrons* 22cm

A small, lightly built coastal tern. Adult appears very white, with grey upperwings showing black tips. Crown black and forehead white, the latter more extensive in winter. Bill yellow with black tip. Immature similar to winter adult but lacking bold head pattern and with grey-brown markings on back and wings. Flight distinctively flicking, but nevertheless strong. Gregarious. Utters high-pitched 'kree-ik' and hurried 'kirri-kirri-kirrick'. Nests colonially on shingle and sandy beaches, occasionally inland. Feeds in shallow inshore seas and lagoons by plunge-diving. Widespread but nowhere numerous.

Sandwich Tern *Sterna sandvicensis* 40cm

 A medium-sized, long-billed tern. Summer adult predominantly white, with grey upperwings and shaggy-crested black crown. Tail white and forked. Bill black with yellow tip, and legs black. Winter adult has white forehead and grey-flecked crown. Immature similar to winter adult, but with grey-brown, scaly appearance to back. Flight buoyant and powerful. Gregarious. Call a harsh and distinctive, disyllabic 'kay-wreck'. Breeds colonially on sandy and shingle beaches, and islands. Feeds at sea by plunge-diving. Migrates through coastal water, often arriving in north-west Europe as early as March. Locally fairly common.

Common Tern *Sterna hirundo* 35cm

 A medium-sized tern. Summer adult largely white, with black cap and greyish upperwings with appreciably darker tips. Tail white and deeply forked. Bill red with black tip and legs red. Winter adult has white forehead. Immature darker, with sandy grey markings on back and wings. Gregarious. Call a harsh 'kee-aarh', with emphasis on second syllable. Nests colonially on coastal beaches, islands, and inland on sand or gravel beside freshwater. Feeds over coastal lagoons, inshore coastal waters and inland lakes, by plunge-diving. Widespread and common at breeding colonies. Also seen on migration around coasts and inland.

Arctic Tern *Sterna paradisaea* 37cm

A medium-sized, elegant tern. Summer adult appears mainly white, with black cap. Upperwings pale grey, distinctively pale and translucent near tips. Tail white, with long streamers. Bill entirely red. Legs red and very short. Winter adult (seldom seen in region) has white forehead with legs and bill dark. Immature similar to winter adult, but with sandy-brown back and wing markings. Call a sharp 'keee-ah', with emphasis on first syllable. Nests colonially on beaches, islands and grassy areas near sea. Feeds by plunge-diving for small fish. Widespread and locally common. Long distance migrant, wintering in Antarctic Ocean.

Razorbill *Alca torda* 40cm

A stockily built, medium-sized seabird. Summer adult jet black above and strikingly white below. Bill large, black and deep, with white vertical line near tip. White line on face from eye to base of bill. Bold, white wingbar conspicuous in flight, as is white trailing edge. Winter adult and immature similar but with greyer plumage and white throat. Utters a gruff growl, usually only on breeding grounds. Breeds on rock-strewn sea cliffs, usually in loose and scattered colonies. Feeds and winters at sea, sometimes in relatively coastal waters. Locally fairly common. Suffers badly from oil pollution at sea.

81

Guillemot *Uria aalge* 40cm

A medium-sized plump-bodied seabird. Summer adult chocolate brown above and white below. Northern birds have much darker upperparts than southern birds. 'Bridled' form has white eye-ring and stripe behind eye, increasingly common in northern latitudes. Bill long, dark and dagger-like. Legs grey. Winter and immature greyer with white faces and throat. Whirring flight low over sea, showing white trailing edge to wing. Appears long and low-bodied while swimming. Dives well. Upright stance on cliffs, where utters various cooing calls. Breeds colonially on cliff ledges, single egg incubated on rock. Winters in coastal seas. Locally common.

Black Guillemot *Cepphus grylle* 33cm

A distinctive, seabird of a medium size. The summer adult is unmistakable. Plumage largely velvet black except for striking white wing patch. Bill black but red inside mouth often visible when calling and displaying. Legs bright vermillion. Winter adult and immature are largely white, but with greyish crown, nape and back. Blackish wings retain the striking white patch. Often seen in pairs or small groups. Utters strange, bell-like twittering calls. Breeds on rocky shores, nesting under boulders. Feeds and winters in adjacent seas, and often faithful to a particular stretch of coast year-round. Local and rarely numerous.

Puffin *Fratercula arctica* 30cm

Easily recognised, medium-sized seabird, the adult unmistakable in summer. Black above and white below, with large white face patch. Huge, parrot-like bill is grey-blue, yellow and red. Legs and feet bright orange-red. Winter adult and immature have smaller, duller bills and grey face patches. Flight whirring, low over sea, no wingbar visible. Gregarious. Utters low growls in breeding season. Breeds on coastal grassy cliffs and scree slopes, nesting in burrow. Breeds colonially, larger colonies with tens of thousands of pairs. Winters mostly far out to sea. Locally numerous, though populations have plummeted in the last decade.

Feral Pigeon and Rock Dove *Columba livia* 33cm

A medium-sized pigeon. Rock Dove is ancestor of familiar, urban Feral Pigeon. Rock Dove is soft grey, adult with metallic sheen on many feathers of nape. In flight, shows white rump and two black bars in rounded wings. Bill dark and stubby and legs reddish. Flight swift and direct. Some Feral Pigeons identical to Rock Dove but many have variable mottled areas of white, buff, orange-brown and black; many lack white rump. Purring and cooing calls. Rock Doves breed on remote rocky coasts and mountainous areas. Feral Pigeons occur in urban areas but may breed in Rock Dove habitats.

Woodpigeon *Columba palumbus* 40cm

A large, cumbersome pigeon. Plumage is delicate grey-brown above and paler dove-grey below. Adult has metallic sheen on nape and conspicuous white collar patches, absent in immature. Bill dull pinkish-orange with white patch at base. Legs pinkish. In flight, white crescent wingbars are striking and diagnostic. Flight is fast but clumsy. Gregarious outside breeding season, often feeding in flocks. Utters a distinctive 'coo-coo-coo, coo-coo'. Breeds in woodland and scrub, building a flimsy, twig nest in fork of tree. Feeds in woodland, farmland and urban areas. The most widespread and common pigeon in the region.

Stock Dove *Columba oenas* 33cm

A medium-sized farmland and woodland pigeon. Superficially similar to Woodpigeon but smaller and slimmer and lacking white on wings or neck. Plumage uniformly dull, leaden grey. Adults have greenish metallic sheen on nape and pinkish flush to breast. In flight, shows distinctive black border to wing, with two, indistinct and irregular black wingbars. Rump grey. Flight swift and direct. Bill short and dark and legs reddish. Gregarious outside breeding season. Utters a repetitive 'coo-ooh', particularly in spring. Nests in holes in trees in farmland and woodland edges, occasionally on coasts. Widespread and locally common.

Turtle Dove *Streptopelia turtur* 28cm

A medium-small pigeon of slim proportions. Adult has back and wings orange-brown, the feathers with dark centres giving almost scaly appearance. Head and neck grey, and underparts pinkish-buff, shading to white on belly. Adult has chequered black and white collar patches. Immature duller and browner, lacking collar markings. Wings dark-tipped and tail blackish, with diagnostic narrow white border visible in flight. Flight swift and direct. Often seen in small flocks. Utters a distinctive and prolonged purring. Occurs in woodland and farmland with hedges and scrub. Widespread and fairly common visitor from May to September.

Collared Dove *Streptopelia decaocto* 28cm

A medium-small, sandy-coloured pigeon. Adult and immature have back and wings sandy brown. Head, neck and underparts appreciably paler pinkish-buff. In flight, wings show dark tips and conspicuous blue-grey forewing patches. Tail brown with broad, white terminal band striking in flight. Black and white crescentic collar band, distinctive in adult and lacking in immature. Sometimes seen in small flocks. Utters a dry 'aaah', usually in flight. Also a strident 'coo coo-coo' delivered from rooftops. Occurs on farmland, parks, gardens and urban areas generally. Widespread and common despite having only recently colonized north-west Europe.

Nightjar *Caprimulgus europaeus* 28cm

This medium-sized nocturnal bird is raptor-like in flight. Plumage rich reddish-brown, beautifully mottled with browns, greys and buff, providing excellent camouflage among fallen leaves or on dead branch. Male has white patches near wingtips and at each side of tip of tail. Eyes huge. Bill tiny but gape huge, used when hunting for flying insects after dark. Flight is strangely silent. During daytime,

sits tight with eyes almost closed, relying on camouflage for protection. Utters a characteristic, continuous churring, augmented by wing-claps in display. It is best located by this distinctive call. Found on heaths, open woodland and scrub. Widespread but only locally common.

Swift *Apus apus* 18cm

The streamlined body and sickle-shaped wings of the Swift are distinctive. Adult sooty black, with greyish throat visible only at close range. Immature brownish-black with pale grey scaly markings. Bill tiny but gape large. Legs tiny and almost useless for walking. Eyes relatively large. Wings long and narrow. Flight is fast and characteristically flickering. Tail short and shallowly forked. Often gregarious. Spends much of life on the wing. Swifts are familiar in many towns, chasing each other overhead while uttering shrill, high-pitched screams. Breeds colonially in urban areas, often under roofs. Feeds almost anywhere. Widespread and locally common.

86

Scop's Owl *Otus scops* 20cm

This small, rather secretive owl is more often heard than seen. Plumage brownish, with two colour phases: reddish-tinged and greyish. Plumage finely marked with grey, black, white and buff. Head shape is distinctive with short, upright 'ear' tufts. Facial disc is oblong and pale grey. Eyes are bright yellow with a dark pupil. Always roosts in well-concealed position during daylight and hunts at night. Daytime roost sometimes given away by distinctive call (heard mostly at night), a penetrating and monotonously repeated 'peeuu', reminiscent of sonar blips. Occurs in open woodland, olive groves and in trees near human habitation such as town parks and gardens. Widespread.

Little Owl *Athene noctua* 23cm

This small, bold owl is often seen perching openly in daylight. Mostly grey-brown above, with bold white spots and streaks. Underparts whitish to grey-buff, heavily streaked with dark brown. Head comparatively large, rounded and flat-crowned. Oblong facial disc greyish with paler margin. Eyes bright yellow with dark pupils. Stance squat but sits upright. Often perches on posts, may bob if approached. Flight undulating and in short bursts. Wings short and rounded. Hunts mainly at dusk and night. Utters various cat-like yelps and penetrating 'poo-oop'. Occurs mainly on farmland, woodland borders and sometimes on coasts. Widespread and locally fairly common.

Long-eared Owl *Asio otus* 35cm

This slim, long-winged, medium-sized owl has unmistakable, bright orange eyes. Entirely nocturnal. Rich brown above with fine markings of black, brown and buff, affording superb camouflage against tree trunk. Underparts rich buff, with bold, dark streaks. Head rounded with conspicuous 'ear' tufts. Facial disc warm buff with black border. Eyes strikingly orange with black pupils. Upright stance, often making body look very slim. In flight, shows relatively long wings with dark patch at 'wrist'. In winter, may roost communally. Mostly silent; utters series of deep 'poop' calls in breeding season. Occurs in woodland, more often coniferous than deciduous. Widespread but never numerous.

Short-eared Owl *Asio flammeus* 38cm

A medium-sized, often diurnal, owl of open country. Upperparts sandy brown with brown and buff markings. Paler below but heavily marked with dark brown streaks. Head rounded with inconspicuous 'ear' tufts. Roughly circular facial disc pale buff with dark border and dark patches around bright yellow eyes. Stance often horizontal. Often hunts in broad daylight, flying low over open ground, with bouncing flight alternating with glides. Underwings pale with conspicuous dark 'wrist' patches. Mostly silent. Occurs in open country including grassy moorland, tundra and marshes. Widespread but numbers unpredictable.

Barn Owl *Tyto alba* 35cm

 A pale, medium-sized owl. Upperparts pale sandy brown, delicately flecked with brown, grey and white. Underparts white in birds from north-western Europe, including Britain and Ireland. Those from southern Europe have underparts rich buff. Facial disc white and characteristically heart-shaped. Eyes dark and large. Stance upright, legs long and 'knock-kneed'. Wings relatively long, appearing very pale in flight. Usually nocturnal but may hunt in daylight in winter. Utters various blood-curdling shrieks while hunting and snoring noises when roosting. Occurs in open woodland, farmland and outskirts of villages. Widespread but nowhere numerous.

Tawny Owl *Strix aluco* 38cm

 A medium-sized, round-headed owl, the commonest in the region. Adult brownish above, varying from chestnut to almost greyish, with fine black streaks and bold buff blotches. Underparts buffish-brown, finely marked with darker brown. Head large and noticeably rounded. Roughly circular facial disc grey-buff with narrow black border. Eyes large and dark. Nocturnal hunter, markedly round-winged in flight. Secretive during day, often revealed by alarm calls of agitated small birds. Heard more often than seen,  uttering the well-known, tremulous 'hoo-hoo-hooo' and a sharp 'kew-wit'. Found in woodland, farmland and urban areas. Widespread although seldom seen.

Kingfisher *Alcedo atthis* 17cm

This rather beautiful bird is unmistakable. Adult has upperparts electric blue-green and dark blue crown with pale blue flecks. Cheeks orange and white, underparts bright orange-brown. Immature slightly duller, with heavily flecked crown. Bill dagger-like and dark, showing reddish base to lower mandible in female. Legs and feet bright scarlet and tiny. Silhouette dumpy with oversized bill and head. Often seen in arrow-like flight on whirring wings low over water. Nests in burrow excavated in sandy bank. Call a shrill, ringing 'cheet'. Occurs on rivers, streams and lakes, occasionally on coasts in winter. Widespread but never numerous, becoming rather scarce.

Bee-eater *Merops apiaster* 28cm

An unmistakable and striking, swallow-like bird. No other European bird possesses such a dazzling array of plumage colours. Adult has upperparts of green, chestnut, yellow and white and underparts yellow, black and turquoise-blue. Immature duller. Tail long, with extended central tail feathers in adult. Bill long, dark and downcurved, and legs short. Flight graceful and agile. Gregarious. In flight, utters characteristic, bell-like 'prewit'. Occurs in open, dry country. Nests in burrows excavated in sandy banks and often feeds over lakes and marshes. Very locally common in southern Europe from May to August. Rare but regular further north.

Roller *Coracias garrulus* 30cm

A medium-sized, unmistakable bird, especially in flight. Adult mostly sky blue with chestnut back. Wings dark brown, with electric blue patches, strikingly obvious in flight. Tail dark blue above, bright blue below. Immature much greyer and duller than adult. Performs characteristic tumbling display flight. Often perches conspicuously on posts or overhead wires. Feeds mainly on insects and reptiles. Call a harsh 'kraak'. Occurs in open bushy, or scrub country, sometimes on farmland. Widespread in southern and eastern Europe from May to August, but seldom numerous. Occurs as rare vagrant further north in Europe.

Hoopoe *Upupa epops* 28cm

This medium-sized, pinkish-fawn and pied bird is unmistakable. Head, neck and breast an unusual and characteristic pinkish-fawn. Has long, black-tipped crest of same colour which is erected when excited or alarmed. Back and wings boldly barred black and white. Tail black with white bar, and belly white. Bill dark, long, slender and slightly downcurved. Legs short. Flight flopping and moth-like. Voice a characteristic, far-carrying and repetitive 'hoo-poo-poo'. Occurs in open country with trees and scrub, such as orchards and olive groves. Widespread but fairly common only in southern Europe.

91

Green Woodpecker *Picus viridis* 30cm

A medium-sized woodpecker. The adult is predominantly yellowish-green above and greenish-buff below. Shows darker barring on flanks. Crown and nape red in both sexes. Dark patch through eye and striking moustachial stripe, black in female, red and black in male. Bill relatively long, grey with dark tip. Immature duller, with reddish crown. Heavily buff-spotted on upperparts and barred on breast and flanks. Often feeds on ground. Flight undulating, showing conspicuous yellow rump. Call a characteristic, ringing laugh 'yah-yah-yah'. Unlike other woodpeckers, it seldom drums. Occurs in open, dry grassland, heaths and rides in deciduous woodland. Widespread.

Great Spotted Woodpecker *Dendrocopus major* 23cm

A smallish, pied woodpecker. Adult boldly marked black and white on upperparts. Forecrown white, crown and nape black, with scarlet nape patch in male only. White cheeks and patches on sides on neck. Underparts whitish with extensive area of red beneath tail. Immature greyer with scarlet crown. Flight undulating, showing bold barring across back, and striking white wing patches. Bill short, stout and black. Utters an explosive 'kek' or 'chack'. Drums frequently. Found in all types of woodland, as well as urban parks and gardens. Nests in hole in tree trunk. Visits bird feeders. Widespread and often fairly common.

Lesser Spotted Woodpecker *Dendrocopus minor* 15cm

A sparrow-sized bird, this is the smallest European woodpecker. Adult and immature predominantly black above, with ladder-like white barring across back. Lacks white wing patches of Great Spotted Woodpecker. Head pattern distinctive with nape black and forehead white. Male has crown red, immature reddish and female white. Underparts, including undertail, whitish and only sparsely streaked. Utters a distinctive and repetitive, shrill 'kee-kee-kee'. Frequent drumming sounds are higher-pitched than the Great Spotted Woodpecker. Occurs in deciduous woods, parks, orchards and olive groves. Widespread but never numerous and easily overlooked.

Wryneck *Jynx torquilla* 18cm

A subdued but beautifully marked bird, with an elongated shape. Related to woodpeckers but atypical of them in its behaviour, plumage and soft tail feathers. Adult and immature brown above, finely mottled and streaked with black and fawn, showing buff 'V' marking. Underparts pale buff with brownish barring. Tail long and brown, with dark barring, not stiff as in other woodpeckers. Bill dark, short and strong. Often feeds on the ground, with ants a favourite food. Call a persistent, laughing 'kee-kee-kee', recalling bird of prey. Found in open woodland, orchards and parkland with old trees. Widespread.

93

Cuckoo *Cuculus canorus* 33cm

This celebrated bird heralds the spring with the familiar call that gave it its name. A slim, long-tailed bird, recalling a medium-sized falcon. Adult dove-grey above, tail long and blackish, with white bars on underside at close range. Underparts white and finely barred grey. Most females are grey; occasional rufous form has rich brown upperparts. Juvenile has upperparts reddish-brown, with dark barring and white on nape. Bill dark with yellow at base. Legs short and yellow. Male utters characteristic 'cuck-oo' as well as rasping chuckle. Female has bubbling trill. Seen in woodland, farmland, moors and marshes. Brood parasite of small birds including Dunnock and Reed Warbler. Widespread and fairly common.

Crested Lark *Galerida cristata* 17cm

A typical lark with a striking crest. Plumage sandy fawn above, tinged chestnut with brown streaking. Underparts pale buffish-white, throat and breast finely streaked with dark brown. Long, brown, dark-streaked crest on crown often held erect. Bill relatively long and brown, legs pale brown. In flight, brown tail with striking chestnut outer feathers. Call a characteristic 'doo-dee-doo'. Song similar to Skylark but usually delivered from ground. Occurs on open land, farms and roadside verges, often near towns. Widespread and common throughout most of mainland Europe but, strangely, extremely rare vagrant to Britain.

Skylark *Alauda arvensis* 18cm

The most common and widespread European lark. Upperparts buffish-brown, feathers with dark centres and pale fringes. Head has dark streaks and bears short crest which is raised when excited. Pale buff eye-stripe extends as pale margin to cheek patch. Underparts pale buff, streaked on breast. Wings dark brown, flight feathers blackish with pale trailing edge. Tail blackish, white edge visible in flight. Juvenile has scaly upperparts. Bill pale brown, legs pinkish-brown. Call a liquid 'chirrup'. Song, musical, varied and often mimetic. Delivered mostly in flight, sometimes for hours. Found on farmland, grassland, moors and heaths. Often abundant.

Woodlark *Lullula arborea* 15cm

A small, short-tailed lark. Upperparts rich brown, with chestnut and buff markings. Crown chestnut with fine black streaks and almost no crest. Conspicuous pale buff eye-stripe over chestnut cheek patch. At rest, wing shows dark spot, bordered with white, on fore-edge. Underparts pale buff, streaked brown on breast. Tail short, chestnut-brown with buff outer feathers. Utters 'tee-loo-ee' call. Song incorporates call-like phrases, often delivered in spiralling song flight. Found in open woodland and heaths, sometimes at quite high elevations. Widespread and locally common in southern Europe. Rather scarce and local further north.

Swallow *Hirundo rustica* 20cm

A small, familiar, highly aerial bird. Adult and immature with upperparts mostly dark glossy blue-black. Shows dark chestnut face patch and white spots on tail, conspicuous in flight. Underparts predominantly white. In flight, wings are slender and curved. Silhouette is slim and long, deeply forked tail bears narrow streamers, longer in adult than immature and longer in male than female. Flight is swift and swooping, catching insects on the wing. Utters a prolonged, musical twittering. Call a sharp 'chirrup'. Nests in farm buildings and in urban areas. Feeds over most habitats. Widespread and common from April to September.

Sand Martin *Riparia riparia* 12cm

A very small swallow-like bird. Adult and immature sandy brown above, immature with pale feather fringes giving scaly appearance. Underparts whitish, with characteristic brown band across breast. Tail brown, short and shallowly forked. Bill and legs small and black. Eyes relatively large. Spends much time on the wing. Gregarious. Utters a soft, rattling trill and a sharp 'chirrup' alarm call. Breeds colonially, nesting in burrows excavated in sandy banks. Often feeds by hawking insects over nearby fresh waters. Widespread and locally numerous. One of the first spring migrants to arrive in northern Europe, sometimes present in late March.

House Martin *Delichon urbica* 12cm

A very small, pied, swallow-like bird. Adult glossy blue-black above with rather duller, blackish flight feathers. In flight, shows diagnostic white rump patch. Tail blue-black and shallowly forked. Underparts white. Legs and toes feathered and white, best observed when collecting mud for nest. Immature greyer, lacking iridescent sheen of adult. Gregarious. Utters unmusical, rattling twitter. Nests colonially on buildings, often in towns, and occasionally on cliffs. Cup-shaped nest built of mud. Feeds over open land and fresh waters, sometimes with Swallows and Sand Martins. Widespread and often numerous from April to September.

Meadow Pipit *Anthus pratensis* 15cm

The most common and widespread pipit in the region. Small, with rather nondescript plumage and superficially wagtail-like structure. Adult and immature brownish above, varying from yellowish through olive to greenish, with abundant dark streaks. Underparts pale grey-buff, shading to whitish on belly, and with dark streaks on breast and flanks. Legs dark brown. Call a thin 'seep'. Song a weak, descending trill, often delivered in parachuting song flight. Occurs on open moorland, grassy heathland, farmland, marshes, and on beaches in winter. Widespread and often common. In winter, sometimes seen feeding in groups.

Tree pipit *Anthus trivialis* 15cm

A typical woodland bird. Identified as a pipit by horizontal stance, longish tail, fine bill and brownish plumage. Adult and immature rich yellow-brown above with plentiful, fine darker brown streaks. Breast buff, shading to white on belly. Conspicuous dark brown streaks on breast and flanks. Rather stockier in build than similar Meadow Pipit. Legs pinkish. Call a distinctive 'tee-zee'. Song a characteristic, descending trill, ending in series of 'see-aah' notes. Usually delivered in song flight, the bird descending on stiffly held wings. Occurs in woodland clearings and wooded heaths. Widespread and locally common from May to August.

Tawny Pipit *Anthus campestris* 17cm

A relatively large, pale pipit. Adult pale, greyish sandy brown above, with faint dark markings. Underparts whitish, breast flushed with pink in spring. Shows conspicuous pale eye-stripe. Immature browner and more heavily marked above, with dark streaking on breast and flanks. Legs pinkish and relatively long for a pipit. Overall, the structure and plumage create a rather wagtail-like appearance. Call a characteristic 'tseep'. Song, often delivered from ground, a repetitive 'seely-seely-seely'. Occurs on dry, often sandy, areas including saltpans, grassland and drying marshes. Widespread and locally fairly common within range.

98

Rock Pipit *Anthus petrosus* 17cm

A largish, dark pipit. Adult and immature largely brownish-grey above, with plentiful dark streaks. Underparts pale grey-buff, with heavy, dark brown markings. Legs grey and relatively long. Long tail is dark with characteristic grey outer feathers. Call a strident 'zeep'. Song a strong, descending trill, often delivered in parachuting display flight. Found on rocky coastlines, including beaches outside breeding season. Almost never seen inland. Widespread but not numerous. WATER PIPIT (*Anthus spinoletta*) is similar, but paler and with fewer dark streaks. Breeds in rocky mountains of mainland Europe but winters in lowland regions, a few in southern Britain.

Yellow Wagtail *Motacilla flava flavissima* 17cm

A comparatively short-tailed, yellowish wagtail. Summer adult male mainly olive-green above with some yellow on nape. Bold yellow eye-stripe separates greenish crown from darker cheek patch. Underparts rich canary yellow. Tail black with white edges. Summer female similar but with yellow less intense and upperparts browner. Winter adult duller, resembling immature with grey-brown upperparts, whitish eye-stripe over dark cheek patch and pale-buff underparts. Often gregarious. Call a rich 'tseep'; song a musical twittering. Occurs in damp meadows, farmland and marshes. Locally common. Several different races in Europe, males having blue, grey or black heads.

Grey Wagtail *Motacilla cinerea* 18cm

The longest-tailed European wagtail, which continually pumps tail up and down. Summer adult male dove-grey above. Bold white eye-stripe separates grey crown from darker cheeks. Lemon-yellow underparts, particularly rich beneath tail. Shows white moustachial stripes and black bib, absent in winter. Female and immature duller with whitish breast and yellow confined to undertail. Tail black with white outer feathers. Call a high-pitched 'chee-seek'. Song 'tsee-tsee-tsee' followed by trill, recalls Blue Tit. Active bird, invariably seen beside water, mainly streams, rivers, rapids and sluices. Widespread and fairly common in suitable habitats.

Pied Wagtail *Motacilla alba yarrellii* 18cm

The most typical wagtail in Britain and Ireland. Summer adult male black above, with black head and breast interrupted by white cheeks and forehead. Underparts white with grey on flanks. Summer female similarly patterned but dark grey on back and wings. Winter male has white, not black, throat. Immature drabber with less distinct patterning. Always active, pumping tail up and down. Call an explosive, disyllabic 'chis-ick'. Twittering song. Found on grassland, farmland and urban areas. Often near water. Common. Replaced in mainland Europe by similar WHITE WAGTAIL (*Motacilla alba alba*) which has grey, not black, back and rump.

100

Red-backed Shrike *Lanius collurio* 18cm

A small but distinctive shrike which preys upon insects and small birds. Adult male has chestnut-brown back with dove-grey nape and crown. Rump grey and tail black with white edges. Black patch through eye. Throat white, rest of underparts white, tinged pinkish-buff. Female dull brown above with a dark brown eye-patch. Underparts whitish, with fine bars. Immature like female, with heavy, scaly markings. Bill dark, relatively large, with hooked tip. Call a harsh 'chack'. Song a melodious warble. Occurs in dryish, open country with bushes or scrub, including heathland. Widespread and fairly common in southern Europe. In Britain, it is effectively extinct as a breeding species but is seen on migration.

Woodchat Shrike *Lanius senator* 18cm

A small, distinctively marked shrike. Adult has white underparts and black back. Black wings have conspicuous double white wing patches. Rump grey and white, tail black with white edges. Crown and nape reddish-chestnut, richer in male than female. Immature sandy brown, with conspicuous scaly markings. Double pale patches on wings and pale rump most noticeable in flight, absent in otherwise similar immature Red-backed Shrike. Utters harsh 'chack' call. Song varied, including musical notes. Occurs in dry, open, bushy country with scattered trees. Locally fairly common in southern Europe. Scarce vagrant northwards to Britain.

Great Grey Shrike *Lanius excubitor* 25cm

 The largest European shrike, recalling a miniature bird of prey. Adult has grey back and black wings with white wingbar, most conspicuous in flight. Tail long and black, with white edges. Crown grey, with narrow white band on forehead, extending over black eye-patch. Underparts whitish. Immature similar, but browner and finely barred on underparts. Bill black and hooked. Utters various harsh calls. Song a jumble of harsh and musical notes. Occurs in open, wooded terrain, and among scrub with taller bushes. Widespread but seldom common. In Britain and north-west Europe, seen as scarce winter visitor from October to March.

Waxwing *Bombycilla garrulus* 17cm

 A Starling-like bird in silhouette and flight. Adult and immature pinkish-brown, slightly paler below than above. Black bib, black eye-patch and chestnut crest. Wings black with white wing bars and yellow margins to flight feathers. Adult has small, wax-like, red feather-ends in wings. Tail blackish with yellow tip. Utters a distinctive, bell-like trill. Breeds in mixed forest and scrub. Precise winter range depends on food supply. Large numbers may move south and west, with many reaching Britain. In winter, may feed on berries in gardens and town parks. Common on breeding grounds but irregular elsewhere.

Golden Oriole *Oriolus oriolus* 25cm

A small bird, Starling-like in structure and profile. Adult male unmistakable with bright, golden-yellow plumage contrasting with black wings. In flight, yellow wingbar and yellow and black tail are conspicuous. Shows black patch through eye and pinkish-red bill. Female and immature yellowish-green above and whitish below, with fine brown streaks on breast and flanks. Secretive and, despite bright colouring, surprisingly difficult to see. Calls are harsh and Starling-like. Song is characteristic, fluting 'wheela-whee-oo'. Song heard more often than bird is seen. Occurs in mature, open deciduous woodland, parks, orchards and olive groves. Widespread.

Starling *Sturnus vulgaris* 22cm

A familiar urban bird. Small, summer adult blackish with glossy iridescence at close range, and buffish flecks on back. Bill yellow with base blue in male and pink in female. Legs pinkish-brown. Winter adult has dark bill, lacks iridescence and is heavily spotted with white. Immature uniformly drab brown. Gregarious, often in huge flocks outside breeding season. Flight swift and direct, with characteristic triangular wing silhouette. Utters various harsh, scolding calls. Song extended and varied, including mimicry of other birds and noises including car alarms and ringing phones. Occurs in wide variety of habitats, often abundant in towns.

103

Jay *Garrulus glandarius* 35cm

A medium-sized, brightly coloured member of the crow family. Upperparts pinkish-buff with chestnut shading, underparts are paler. White rump and black tail noticeable in flight, which is floppy, on erratically beating, rounded wings. Crown pinkish with black flecks, raised as a short crest if excited. Shows black moustachial stripes, pale pink eyes and dark grey bill. Wings blackish with bold, white wingbar and bright chequered blue patch at 'wrist'. Often rather wary, uttering harsh 'skaark' call. Rarely heard song a subdued mixture of cackling notes. Occurs in woods, farmland and parkland with plentiful trees. Widespread and often quite common.

Magpie *Pica pica* 45cm

An unmistakable, long-tailed, pied member of the crow family. Head and nape glossy black, back and upper breast dull black. Belly white, wings black and white. Long, rather tapering tail is black with glossy purple and green iridescence. Freshly fledged immature duller, with rather shorter tail. Flight direct, but on fluttering, rounded wings. Call a harsh, rattling chatter. Song, seldom heard, a quiet but surprisingly musical collection of piping notes. Occurs in woodland, parkland, farmland, heath, scrub and mature gardens. Sometimes even in city-centre parks. Widespread and locally numerous but persecuted in some areas.

Chough *Pyrrhocorax pyrrhocorax* 37cm

A medium-sized member of the crow family with a slim, red bill. Adult plumage wholly glossy black, with iridescent sheen. Legs distinctive and contrasting deep red. Bill crimson, relatively long, slender and down-curved. Immature rather dull, sooty brown, with brown legs and rather shorter, orange bill. Aerobatic, swooping about in air currents near cliff faces on rounded, heavily fingered wings. Often seen in parties of ten or more birds. Very vocal, calls including a distinctive 'chee-ow' and a sharp 'krish'. Occurs in rocky mountainous areas, coastal cliffs and crags. Locally common, especially in southern Europe from Spain to Greece.

Alpine Chough *Pyrrhocorax graculus* 37cm

A medium-sized member of the crow family with a slim yellow bill. Adult plumage wholly black. Legs bright coral red, bill slender and yellow. Immature dull sooty-grey with blackish legs. Aerobatic, swooping and tumbling in air currents on rounded, heavily fingered wings. Very vocal, uttering a loud, echoing 'chee-up' or thin 'skree'. Occurs in alpine areas at far greater altitudes than the Chough, often well above the snow line. Scavenges around summit stations of ski-lifts, sometimes lower down in winter. Parties of birds appear from nowhere at slightest hint of food scraps. Locally common within restricted range.

Jackdaw *Corvus monedula* 33cm

This is the smallest and commonest member of the crow family in Europe. Adult and immature have most of head and body dull sooty black, with variable amounts of grey on crown, nape and upper breast. Bill relatively short, but rather stout. Adult has startlingly white eye, duller in immature. Flight usually direct, with quicker wingbeats than other crows, and lacking fingered wingtips. Gregarious, often in large flocks and sometimes along with Rooks. Vocal, uttering a metallic 'jack' call. Occurs in open woodland, parkland and farmland, and in churches and houses in urban areas. Often nests colonially in old trees or ruined buildings. Widespread and often common.

Rook *Corvus frugilegus* 45cm

A medium-large member of the crow family. Adult plumage wholly glossy black, with iridescent sheen. Feathers of upper leg ('thigh') loose and rough, giving 'baggy trousered' appearance. Bill pale, long and dagger-shaped, rather rough textured and running to whitish cheek patches. Immature duller sooty black with blackish bill. Lacks cheek patches. Colonial when breeding, nesting in tree tops, and gregarious at other times. Often feeds alongside Jackdaws. Vocal and noisy, uttering raucous 'carr' call. Occurs in arable farmland with adjacent woodland or plenty of tall trees for nesting. Widespread and often common.

106

Carrion Crow *Corvus corone corone* 45cm

 A largish crow. Adult and immature plumage wholly black. Bill black and stout, with convex upper mandible and black feathers at base. Feathers of upper leg ('thigh') neatly close-fitting. Usually solitary and only occasionally gregarious. Call a deep, harsh 'caw' or 'corr'. Occurs in open countryside of all types with suitable tall trees for nesting. Also sometimes in urban areas and even city centres. Widespread but rarely very numerous. Closely related subspecies HOODED CROW (*Corvus corone cornix*) has more north-easterly distribution in Europe but distributions overlap. Plumage black except for grey back, breast and belly.

Raven *Corvus corax* 63cm

 The largest member of the crow family in Europe. Plumage wholly black, with iridescent sheen in adult, lacking in immature. Wings broad and long, with heavily fingered tips. Tail relatively long and characteristically wedge-shaped. Head appears heavy, with bristling throat feathers and massive angular bill. Despite size, very aerobatic, riding upcurrents off cliff faces. Performs tumbling and rolling displays, especially in spring. Rarely gregarious although often seen in pairs. Call a distinctive, deep, gruff croak or 'gronk'. Occurs on rocky coasts and mountain and moorland crags. Widespread but nowhere numerous.

Dipper *Cinclus cinclus* 17cm

A small and dumpy bird which resembles a thrush-sized Wren. Adult rich dark brown above with striking white throat and breast. Belly rich chestnut in birds from Britain and Ireland. Mainland European birds have a black breast. Immature scaly grey, darker above than below. Flight fast, whirring and low over water. Often seen standing on rocks in rivers, bobbing incessantly before plunging into water to feed on larvae from the riverbed. Call a loud 'zit' and song a fragmented warbling. Found on fast-flowing, clear rivers in hilly country. Very occasionally on margins of lakes or sheltered coasts. Widespread but seldom particularly common because of habitat requirements.

Wren *Troglodytes troglodytes* 10cm

This is one of the smallest European birds. Adult and immature a rich chestnut-brown, barred with dark brown above. Underparts rather paler with less barring. Tail narrow and characteristically carried cocked upright. Bill thin and needle-like. Flight low and direct, on short, rounded, whirring wings. Seldom flies for any great distance. Call a scolding 'churr'; song musical, extended and astonishingly loud for a bird of this size. Occurs in well-vegetated habitats of all kinds, from cliff sides to woodland rides and heaths to mountain screes. Widespread and often common, although numbers plummet during severe winters.

Dunnock *Prunella modularis* 15cm

A small and rather drab bird of the undergrowth. Superficially sparrow-like but with fine bill. Adult has rich brown upperparts with darker markings. Head, nape and breast distinctive leaden grey and belly buff. Sexes similar. Immature more subdued with speckled upperparts and lacks grey. Call a thin, shrill 'seek'. Song a short, suddenly interrupted, melodious warble, somewhat reminiscent of Blackcap's song. Found in tangled undergrowth and scrub associated with woodland of all types, farmland, town parks and gardens. Widespread and locally common but easy to overlook due to unobtrusive habits.

Grasshopper Warbler *Locustella naevia* 13cm

A tiny, dark-streaked warbler similar to Sedge Warbler. Adult and immature have upperparts dull grey-brown with dense, darker brown streaks. Underparts greyish-buff, often spotted on throat, paling to near-white on belly. Greyish eye-stripe. Tail brown with wedge-shaped tip. Extremely secretive, normally moving through cover rather than flying. Heard far more often than actually seen. Song, often delivered at night, a high-pitched, reeling trill, often of many minutes' duration. Sounds ventriloquial. Sometimes sings from exposed perch. Occurs in areas of dense, shrubby vegetation, ranging from reedbeds to young plantations. Widespread but rarely numerous.

Sedge Warbler *Acrocephalus schoenobaenus* 13cm

 This small, heavily streaked warbler is typical of waterside habitats. Back is olive-brown and heavily streaked with blackish-brown. Crown brown, with narrow blackish stripes, separated from grey-brown cheeks by clear whitish eye-stripe. Underparts whitish, tinged buff on flanks. Tail brown, tinged chestnut. Inquisitive. Rarely flies far in the open. Utters an explosive 'tuck' in alarm. Song comprises a rapid, repetitive, grating jingle, interspersed with chattering notes. Sometimes delivered in short, vertical song flight but more usually from bush or reed. Occurs in reedbeds and adjacent shrubby swamps. Widespread and often common in suitable habitats.

Fan-tailed Warbler *Cisticola juncidis* 10cm

 This extremely small, heavily streaked warbler is best known for its distinctive song and for its mode of delivery. Upperparts buffish-brown, heavily streaked with dark brown. Underparts paler greyish-fawn and lightly streaked. Tail grey-brown, very short and rounded. Often flicked in Wren-like manner. Secretive, except in song flight, flying short distances on short rounded and whirring wings. Song a plaintive 'zip-zip-zip' delivered in yo-yo-like song flight. Occurs on both wet and dry open areas such as dense marshy clumps, grain fields and grassy plains. Non-migratory. Locally fairly common. Breeds on French coast, ye very rare vagrant to Britain.

Reed Warbler *Acrocephalus scirpaceus* 13cm

This small, unstreaked warbler is typical of wetland habitats. Upperparts rich reddish-brown, lacking darker streaks of Sedge Warbler. Shows faint, buffish eye-stripe. Underparts whitish, shading to buff on flanks. Tail reddish-brown, relatively long and tapered towards tip. Legs normally dark brown. Utters a 'churr' alarm call. Song prolonged and repetitive, with spells of chirruping. More musical and less twangy than Sedge Warbler, often with some mimicry. Usually delivered from cover. Typically found in reedbeds but sometimes in other heavily vegetated freshwater margins. Widespread and often common from May to August.

Melodious Warbler *Hippolais polyglotta* 13cm

This small warbler has a relatively large, stout bill compared with similar-sized warblers. Upperparts are greyish-green, showing rich yellow eye-stripe. Underparts yellowish. Plumage generally brighter in juvenile than adult. Wings and tail brown and uniform. At rest, wingtips extend to base of tail. Bill long and broad, legs brownish. Utters sparrow-like chattering and soft 'hoo-eet' call. Song extended, slow initially then rapid and melodious. Occurs in woodland undergrowth, parks and gardens. Locally common. ICTERINE WARBLER (*Hippolais icterina*) is similar, occurring in eastern Europe. At rest, wings extend halfway down tail and show pale panel.

111

Garden Warbler *Sylvia borin* 15cm

This small warbler lacks distinctive features. Plumage characteristically drab greyish-olive above. Underparts whitish, shaded grey or buff, especially on flanks. Faint pale eye-stripe and bluish-grey legs. Rather secretive and retiring. Call a sharp 'tack'. Song an extended, liquid, melodious warbling, usually delivered from deep cover. Can sound rather similar to song of Blackcap. Occurs in well-grown, thick scrub or dense woodland undergrowth. Tall trees appear not to be a necessary habitat requirement, unlike Blackcap. Widespread and occasionally quite common from May to August. Easily overlooked unless singing.

Blackcap *Sylvia atricapilla* 15cm

A small warbler, with the sexes having different plumages. Male has greyish-olive upperparts, pale grey underparts and characteristic black crown. Female and immature have grey-brown upperparts, pale grey underparts with cap brown in female and ginger-chestnut in immature. Legs bluish-grey. Call a sharp 'tack'. Song a melodious warble, similar but briefer than Garden Warbler, usually ending in rising notes. Occurs in parks, mature gardens and woodland, with both well-developed undergrowth and tall trees. Widespread and locally quite common from May to August. A few birds overwinter in north-west Europe but mostly summer visitor.

Whitethroat *Sylvia communis* 14cm

 A small, active warbler. Adult male has grey-brown upperparts with characteristic pale chestnut wings and white-edged, dull brown tail. Throat strikingly white, rest of underparts looking rather dingy white in comparison, tinged pinkish-buff. Female and immature browner and paler, but with chestnut wings still evident. Legs brownish. Active, but fairly secretive except in song. Call a rasping and scolding 'tschack'. Song a rapid and scratchy warble, usually delivered in song flight. Occurs on scrubby hillsides and maquis, more occasionally on heaths and in woodland clearings. Widespread and locally common from May to August.

Lesser Whitethroat *Sylvia curruca* 13cm

 A small, rather dull-looking warbler. Adult has upperparts largely grey-brown, with brown wings and white-edged tail. Crown grey, with distinctive blackish patch through eye and ear coverts. Underparts white, tinged pink on breast and flanks in early summer. Legs bluish-grey. Immature duller, lacking pink flush on underparts. Rather secretive and skulking. Call a short 'tack'. Song a brief warble, followed by repetitive rattle on single note. Very distinctive once learned and best clue as to bird's presence. Occurs in farmland hedges, woodland clearings and scrubby hillsides. Widespread but seldom numerous. Occurs from May to August.

113

Sardinian Warbler *Sylvia melanocephala* 13cm

A small, distinctive warbler with a reddish eye-ring, brighter in the male than the female. Adult male has grey upperparts and distinctive black head. Underparts white, strikingly so on throat, shading to grey on flanks. Tail almost black, with white edges. Legs brown. Female and immature, considerably duller and browner, with cap similar colour to mantle and eye-ring brownish. Secretive but active. Call a scolding chatter. Song an extended, scratchy warble interspersed with melodious phrases. Often delivered in bouncing song flight. Occurs in scrub, maquis and bush-covered rocky hillsides. Widespread in Mediterranean region and often common.

Subalpine Warbler *Sylvia cantillans* 13cm

A small, attractively marked warbler. Adult male dark grey above, but not as dark as Dartford Warbler. Wings dark brown and tail dark brown with white edges. Throat and breast chestnut red, with white moustachial stripe. Belly white. Female and immature much less richly coloured than male and moustachial stripe often hard to detect. Legs brown. Secretive and rather skulking. Call a sharp 'tchack'. Song a brief, musical warble, lacking harsh, metallic notes. Often delivered in song flight. Occurs in arid scrub, heath, maquis and woodland clearings. Locally fairly common within range. Very rare vagrant further north in Europe.

Dartford Warbler *Sylvia cantillans* 13cm

A tiny, dark, long-tailed warbler. Adult dark grey above with underparts characteristically dark red with white flecks, paling to white beneath tail. Tail long and dark grey, often held cocked. Red eye-ring and chestnut eye visible at close range. Legs brownish. Immature dull brown above, grey-buff below. Usually rather secretive but sometimes perches momentarily on top of gorse bush when agitated. Utters a buzzing, metallic 'tchurr-tchit' call. Song a quiet, brief, scratchy warble. Occurs on dry heathland with tall gorse bushes and maquis. Locally common in mainland Europe. In Britain, very local on southern heathland.

Willow Warbler *Phylloscopus trochilus* 10cm

This tiny leaf warbler has a distinctive song. Adult and immature pale olive-green above, with clear pale eye-stripe. Underparts whitish, strongly tinged with yellow in immature, especially on flanks. Legs usually brown. Call a plaintive 'hoo-eet'. Song a characteristic, melodious, silvery, descending warble with a final flourish. Quite unlike that of superficially similar Chiffchaff. Occurs in woodlands with dense undergrowth, heathland with birch trees, and parkland. At far north of range, found in scrub without trees. Widespread and common. One of the first migrants to arrive in Europe in the spring. Song often heard by early April.

Chiffchaff *Phylloscopus collybita* 10cm

This tiny, rather drab leaf warbler has a distinctive song. Adult and immature drab brownish-olive above. Underparts whitish, shaded to buff on flanks and often yellow-tinged in immature. Brown wings lack wingbars and tail brown. Pale yellow eye-stripe. Legs usually blackish. Call a plaintive 'hoo-eet', similar to Willow Warbler. Song, however, is striking and diagnostic, a monotonous series of 'chiff-chaff' notes. Favours mature woodlands, with both tall trees and well-developed undergrowth. Rarely occurs in scrub, except on migration. Widespread and often common. In Britain, arrives early and often starts singing by late March.

Wood Warbler *Phylloscopus sibilatrix* 13cm

A small, but one of the larger, leaf warblers with bright plumage. Adult and immature have upperparts yellowish-olive and distinct yellowish eye-stripe. Face, throat and breast are rich yellow, rest of underparts are strikingly white. Brown wings lack wingbars but show yellowish feather fringes. Legs pale pinkish-brown. Utters a liquid 'dee-you' call. Song is a characteristic trill, based on accelerating repetition of 'sip' notes. Has been likened to silver sixpence spinning on a plate. Sometimes delivered in song flight. Occurs in mature deciduous woodland, often beech, usually with comparatively little undergrowth. Widespread and very locally common.

Goldcrest *Regulus regulus* 9cm

One of the smallest European birds. Adult and immature have olive-green upperparts and whitish underparts. Tail short and brown, wings brownish with double white wingbar. Head pattern is characteristic, with crown-stripe yellowish-gold in female, flame-coloured in male, broadly edged in black. Head shows diffuse white eye-ring. Immature has plain head. Bill, short, dark and finely pointed. Legs dark brown. Utters a thin, very high-pitched 'tsee' call. Song a high-pitched, descending series of 'tsee-tsee-tsee' notes, terminating in a flourishing trill. Occurs in woodland, occasionally in parks and gardens. Widespread and often common.

Pied Flycatcher *Ficedula hypoleuca* 13cm

This small, compact flycatcher has noticeably pied plumage. Summer adult male has black upperparts with bold white wingbars and white patch on forehead. Year-old males may have brownish wings and tail. Tail black with white edges, frequently flicked. Underparts white. Winter male (seen occasionally on migrating birds in autumn), female and immature are brown above and white below, with grey-buff shading. Call a sharp 'wit'. Song an unmelodious series of rattling notes. Occurs in rather open, mature woodland, usually deciduous, with scant undergrowth. Will breed in nestboxes. Locally common from May to July.

Spotted Flycatcher *Muscicapa striata* 15cm

A small, elongated flycatcher, which often adopts a rather upright pose. Adult and immature drab brown above, with dark brown, closely spaced streaks on crown. Underparts buffish, shading to white on belly, with brown streaking on breast. Immatures have pale scaly markings on back when freshly fledged. Flight characteristic, dashing out from prominent perch to catch insect prey, usually returning to same perch. Shows relatively long wings and tail. Call a sharp 'zit'. Song a brief sequence of squeaky notes. Found in woodland clearings, scrub, farmland, parks and mature gardens with plenty of trees. Widespread and fairly common.

Wheatear *Oenanthe oenanthe* 15cm

A small, pale, compact member of the chat family with a white rump. Summer male has pale grey upperparts, black patch through eye and ear coverts, and blackish wings. Tail black with white rump and base of tail, striking in flight. Underparts dull orange-buff. Winter male browner. Female grey-brown above, buff below, with brown patch through eye and ear coverts. Immature similar, copiously speckled with buff. Largely terrestrial, runs in short bursts, then pauses with tail cocked. Call a harsh 'tack'. Song a brief, scratchy warble. Occurs on open areas of heath, grassland or moorland. Widespread, only locally common.

118

Black-eared Wheatear *Oenanthe hispanica* 15cm

A small, terrestrial member of the chat family. Superficially similar to Wheatear but slimmer, appears almost black and white in bright light. Adult male pale cinnamon-brown, with black wings and prominent white rump, best seen in flight. Two races: male of one has large patch through eye; other has completely black face and throat. Winter male much duller. Female and immature similar to Wheatear but with darker cheeks and wings. Similar in both races. Call a harsh 'tchack'; song a high-pitched, scratchy warble. Occurs in dry, open, often stony areas with little tall vegetation. Locally common within range.

Whinchat *Saxicola rubetra* 13cm

A small, upright member of the chat family. Summer adult male speckled brown and fawn above. Bold white eye-stripe separates crown from characteristic dark cheek patch. Tail dark brown, shows white markings at base in flight. Underparts pale orange. Wings and tail constantly flicked. Winter male appreciably duller. Female paler and duller than male. Immature paler and duller still, heavily streaked on underparts. Call a harsh 'teck'. Song, a short, high-pitched warble, often delivered in song flight. Occurs on open grassland, heaths and scrub. Widespread, only locally numerous.

119

This small, upright, noisy member of the chat family is widespread. In summer adult male has dark brown back, pale rump and black tail. Head and throat black, white patches on side of neck. Breast orange-buff, shading towards white on belly. Winter male similar, colour obscured by pale feather fringes. Female similar, but browner and heavily streaked. Lacks pale rump. Immature brown above and paler below, copiously buff-speckled. Perches on bushes, with wings and tail flicking. Call a sharp 'tchack', like two pebbles knocked together. Song is a high-pitched, scratchy warble. Occurs on heaths, grassland and scrub, often with gorse. Locally common.

Rock Thrush *Monticola saxatilis* 20cm

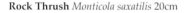

An attractive and colourful southern European thrush. Summer adult male unmistakable. Head, nape, breast and rump blue. White lower back striking in flight. Wings black, belly and tail chestnut. Female, winter male and immature altogether drabber but retain chestnut tail. Upperparts brown and underparts buff with copious dark, scaly markings. Largely terrestrial. As name implies, often associated with rocks and boulder scree. Call a brief 'tack'. Song, a varied and fluting warble. Found mostly at high altitudes in mountainous areas. Widespread but rarely common. Present from May to August. Very rare vagrant north of usual breeding range.

Blue Rock Thrush *Monticola solitarius* 20cm

This dark thrush is typical of the Mediterranean region. Summer adult male unmistakable with head and body characteristic slate blue. Wings and tail blackish. Female and immature duller with brown upperparts and fawn underparts with copious speckling. Largely terrestrial. Wary and often very shy, disappearing among rocks if disturbed. Call a harsh 'tchick'. Song, loud and musical, often delivered from prominent rocky perch, overlooking territory. Occurs in rocky or mountainous areas. Often on the coast, especially in winter, and more occasionally in towns. Always found at lower altitudes than Rock Thrush. Widespread but rarely numerous.

Redstart *Phoenicurus phoenicurus* 15cm

A small, red-tailed member of the chat family. Summer adult male unmistakable. Strikingly pale, blue-grey above, with white forehead and characteristic reddish-chestnut tail. Face and throat black, breast bright chestnut and belly white. Winter adult male browner and less distinctively marked, due to pale feather fringes. Female has brown upperparts, fawn underparts and reddish tail. Immature browner above, paler below and copiously buff-flecked like immature Robin, but with chestnut tail. Call a melodious 'tu-eet'. Song, a brief, melodious warble ending in a dry rattle. Found in woodlands and sometimes in scrub. Widespread and locally common.

121

Black Redstart *Phoenicurus ochruros* 15cm

A small, mostly dark member of the chat family with a reddish tail, striking in flight. Summer adult male dark ash-grey above, with sooty black on face and breast. Belly white, rump and tail (often flicked) chestnut red. White wingbar can be striking in older birds. Winter male duller, retains reddish tail. Female uniformly drab, dark grey-brown, still with reddish tail. Immature dark brown with copious paler spots and reddish tail. Call a sharp 'tick'. Song, a rapid but brief, rattling warble. Occurs in mountain screes and, especially in north-west Europe, in urban sites. Widespread and locally common.

Bluethroat *Luscinia svecica* 15cm

Easily distinguished by its blue throat, this secretive bird is the size and shape of a Robin. Summer adult male has bright blue throat and breast, fringed with black and chestnut. Central spot white in southern race or red in northern race. Upperparts brown. Characteristic chestnut patches on each side of base of tail seen best in flight. At other seasons, male similar, but duller. Female similar but has white throat, fringed with black. Immature resembles slim immature Robin, but distinguished by chestnut tail markings. Call a sharp 'tack'. Song, a high-pitched, melodious warble. Occurs in northern swamps, heathland bogs and marshes. Locally fairly common.

Robin *Erithacus rubecula* 13cm

In Britain, a familiar garden bird. Adult predominantly sandy grey-brown above, with orange-red face, throat and breast, broadly edged with dark grey. Grey on lower breast extensive, shading to white on belly. Narrow, buff wingbars conspicuous in perched bird but not striking in flight. Tail unmarked sandy brown. Immature darker brown above. Underparts pale buff, copiously speckled and barred. Call a sharp 'tick'. Song, a high-pitched, rambling warble, often heard with less intensity outside breeding season. Occurs in woods, parks and urban areas. Sometimes becomes very tame. Widespread and common.

Nightingale *Luscinia megarhynchos* 17cm

This small, rather drab, thrush-like bird is an incomparable songster. Adult olive-brown above, with long, round-ended, rufous tail. Underparts pale buff and unmarked, almost white on belly. Immature sandy brown above, paler below and copiously spotted, but with long, rufous tail. Legs relatively long and powerful, suited to terrestrial habits. Call a soft 'hoo-eet'. Song is long, loud and melodious, richly varied and containing some mimicry of other birds. Often delivered day and night. Occurs in dense woodland undergrowth and swampy thickets. In Britain, prefers coppiced woodland. Widespread and locally common.

123

Ring Ouzel *Turdus torquatus* 25cm

The mountain equivalent of the Blackbird. Summer adult male unmistakable. Plumage largely sooty black, with bold white crescentic patch on breast. Winter male greyer, with white patch smudged sooty-grey. Female largely brown with darker speckling, the pale buff, crescentic bib sometimes poorly marked. Immature brown with paler, scaly markings and lacking bib. In flight, wings appear pale grey, a useful distinguishing feature from Blackbird. Call a characteristic 'chack'. Song loud, repetitive, echoing 'chew-chew-chew'. Occurs on moorland and mountainsides, especially near rocky ravines. Seen on migration around coasts. Widespread but never numerous.

Blackbird *Turdus merula* 25cm

One of the best-known British birds. The male is unmistakable, with entirely glossy, velvet black plumage and contrasting orange bill and eye-ring. Tail dark and comparatively long. Female dark brown above and paler below, with dark-bordered whitish throat. Bill dark, with trace of yellow at base. Immature rather more ginger brown than female and heavily buff-spotted. Call a loud 'chink' or 'chack', often persistent when alarmed by predator. Song fluting, varied, extended and melodious. Occurs on farmland, woodland and urban areas and is a well-known garden bird in most of Europe. Widespread and often abundant. Mostly a year-round resident.

Song Thrush *Turdus philomelos* 23cm

A smallish, short-tailed, upright thrush. Adult olive or sandy-brown above, tinged yellowish-buff. Shows pale eye-stripe above darker brown cheek patch. Wing and tail chestnut-brown. Underparts greyish-white, tinged cinnamon, heavily streaked and spotted with dark brown. Immature similar, but with copious yellow-buff speckling on upperparts. In flight, underwings are pale sandy brown. Call a thin 'seep'. Song, a series of musical notes, each repeated two or three times. Often delivered from prominent perch. Found in woods, parks, gardens and farmland with plentiful trees. Widespread and often common. Resident in north-west Europe.

Mistle Thrush *Turdus viscivorus* 27cm

This largish, pale thrush has a relatively long tail. Adult pale grey-brown above with dark brown wings. Tail dark with pale grey-buff outer feathers. Underparts whitish, heavily spotted with brown. In flight, white underwing is conspicuous. Immature greyer, appears much paler because of copious pale scaly feather margins on upperparts. Call an angry, extended rattle. Song simple and slow, but tuneful, often delivered early in spring and sometimes at dusk or during rainfall. Usually delivered from prominent perch. Found in woodland, parks, gardens and farmland with trees. Often in open grassland or berry-bearing bushes in winter. Widespread.

Redwing *Turdus iliacus* 20cm

A small, rather dark thrush. Adult dark russet brown above, with buffish eye-stripe and moustachial stripe on either edge of dark cheek patch. Underparts whitish, with dark brown streaks and reddish flanks. Immature similar but duller, with copious sandy speckling on back. In flight, characteristic red underwing prominent. Usually gregarious in winter, often in company of Fieldfares. Call an extended 'see-eep', sometimes heard at night from migrating birds. Song a slow series of fluting notes. Breeds in northern forests, parks and gardens. Winters in woodland and open farmland, sometimes in gardens during severe weather, Widespread and sometimes numerous.

Fieldfare *Turdus pilaris* 25cm

A comparatively large and attractively marked thrush. Adult has crown, nape and rump dove-grey. Back, mantle and wings are rich golden russet brown. Underparts are whitish, with heavy black and orange-buff feathering on breast and flanks. Immature browner above. Underparts fawn and heavily speckled. Usually gregarious outside the breeding season. Call a very characteristic series of laughing 'chacks', sometimes heard from migrating birds at night. Song a scratchy warble. Breeds in northern forests, parks and gardens. In winter, found on open farmland, hedgerows and open woodland. Sometimes visits gardens during severe winter weather. Widespread and often common.

Long-tailed Tit *Aegithalos caudatus* 15cm

A small, lively tit with a fluffy body and a very long tail. Upperparts white and brown, tinged pink. Head white with dark stripes over eyes, but all-white in northern race. Bill black, short and stubby. Tail blackish with white outer edges to feathers. Underparts white, tinged pale buffish-pink on belly and flanks. Wings short and rounded. Flight feeble. Often in roving, noisy flocks, sometimes with other species. Calls include a thin 'see' and a churring 'tchurr'. Song, rarely heard, a subdued mixture of call-like notes. Occurs in woodland undergrowth, scrub, heathland and farmland hedges. Widespread and often common.

Marsh Tit *Parus palustris* 13cm

Does not, as its name suggests, frequent marshes. Sombre-coloured, brownish tit. Adult and immature uniform olive-brown above, wings and tail slightly darker brown. Crown and nape glossy black, contrasting with whitish cheeks. Underparts largely greyish-buff, with small black bib on throat. Call, a diagnostic, explosive 'pit-chew', a good feature for separation from similar Willow Tit. Song, a bell-like note, repeated several times, or sometimes 'pitchaweeoo' and other variants of call. Found in woodland, usually deciduous or mixed, with abundant undergrowth. Also in scrub, parkland and mature gardens, where sometimes visits bird feeders. Widespread but rarely numerous.

Willow Tit *Parus montanus* 13cm

This small, sombre, brownish tit is superficially very similar to the Marsh Tit. Adult and immature uniformly brown above with dark brown tail. Wings dark brown, often showing pale central panel. Crown and nape matt black, contrasting with whitish cheeks which are strikingly white in northern race. Underparts largely greyish-buff. Black bib appreciably larger than in Marsh Tit. Call a thin, nasal 'dee-dee-dee' or 'zee-zee': the best feature for separation from Marsh Tit. Song liquid and warbling, but seldom heard. Found in shrubby woodland, scrub and gardens, often favouring damp areas. Widespread but rarely numerous.

Blue Tit *Parus caeruleus* 12cm

A familiar and engaging, tiny tit. Adult has greenish back and characteristic bright blue wings and tail. Head white, with bright blue crown, black line through eye and black bib. Underparts yellow. Male shows brighter blues than female. Immature less well-marked, with greenish upperparts and lacking blue crown until autumn. Calls varied, but 'tsee-tsee-tsee-sit' often used. Song a fast trill, opening with series of 'tsee' notes. Found in a wide variety of habitats, ranging from woodland of all sorts to urban gardens, farmland and even marshland in winter. Visits bird feeders. Widespread and often numerous.

Great Tit *Parus major* 15cm

The largest of the tits. Adult has greenish back, blue-grey wings with white wingbars, and blackish tail with conspicuous white edges. Crown and nape glossy black, with striking white cheeks and indistinct whitish nape patch. Breast and belly yellow, with central black stripe broader in male than female. Immature duller and greener, with grey-green rather than black markings. Feeds more often on ground than other tits. Calls extremely varied, but 'tchink' common. Song characteristically repetitive, ringing 'tea-cher, tea-cher'. Found in woodland of all types, farmland, parks and gardens. Widespread and often numerous.

Coal Tit *Parus ater* 12cm

A tiny, highly active and gregarious tit. Adult and immature olive-grey above, with glossy black head and bib relieved by contrasting white patches on cheeks and nape. Underparts pale buff, with richer cinnamon tones on flanks. Pale feather tips form two whitish wingbars, easily visible at rest. Call a high-pitched, plaintive 'tseet'. Song a high-pitched, repetitive 'wheat-see, wheat-see'. In winter, often in roving mixed flocks of woodland birds. Occurs in woods, hedges, heaths, gardens and in woodland of all types, but favours conifers. Also in parks and gardens, visits bird feeders for peanuts. Widespread and often common throughout the region.

Crested Tit *Parus cristatus* 12cm

Small and active, this is Europe's only tit with a crest. Adult and immature uniformly brown above and uniformly pale buff below. Head pattern characteristic. White face has black lines on nape and cheeks, and shows broad, black bib. Crest long and chequered in black and white. Call a characteristic purring trill. Song a high-pitched, repetitive mixture of 'tsee' notes. Often feeds high in trees. Occurs in mixed or coniferous woodland. Nests in hole in decaying tree stumps. In Britain, confined to ancient pine forests in Scotland. Widespread and locally fairly common in mainland Europe, rather scarce in Britain.

Nuthatch *Sitta europaea* 15cm

A diminutive, woodpecker-like bird of woodland. Adult and immature distinctive blue-grey above, the wings dark grey. White-tipped tail is dove-grey. Shows black eye-stripe. Throat white, rest of underparts pale buff, shading to cinnamon on flanks in female, and chestnut in male. Northern race almost white below. Bill long and dagger-like. Moves actively on trunks and branches, tail up and head down. The only bird which regularly walks head-first down tree trunks. Call a far-carrying, ringing 'chwit'. Song is a 'toowee-toowee'. Occurs in deciduous woodland and parkland, occasionally in gardens. Widespread and locally common.

Treecreeper *Certhia familiaris* 12cm

As its name suggests, a tree-climbing woodland bird. Adult and immature dark brown above, densely streaked white. Shows whitish eye-stripe over darker brown cheek patch. Underparts whitish, often stained and grubby due to contact with bark. Tail long and brown, with central feathers pointed. Bill long, pointed and downcurved. Flight undulating, showing multiple wingbars. Creeps like a mouse up tree trunks, searching for insects. Then flies to base of adjacent trunk to repeat the process. Call a thin, shrill 'tseeu'. Song high-pitched and descending, with final flourish. Occurs in mature woodland, often with conifers. Widespread but rarely numerous.

House Sparrow *Passer domesticus* 15cm

A familiar bird of urban settings. Adult male has rich brown back, with darker streaks, and grey rump. Wings brown with double wingbar. Cheeks whitish, crown grey and nape rich, dark chestnut. Throat and upper breast black, rest of underparts whitish. Tail blackish. Female and immature sandy brown above, with darker brown markings, and clear buff eye-stripe. Underparts pale grey-buff. Bill brownish in female, blackish in male. Gregarious. Noisy, uttering a clear 'chirrup' call. Song a monotonous series of chirruping notes. Invariably associated with man, particularly around farms, but also in towns and cities. Widespread and often numerous.

Tree Sparrow *Passer montanus* 13cm

A superficially similar bird to the House Sparrow, but it is less strongly associated with man. Sexes similar with upperparts brown, mottled with black streaks. Crown and nape chestnut, cheeks white with central black spot. Shows small black bib with rest of underparts off-white. Immature drabber and less clearly marked. Bill stubby and black. Gregarious. In eastern Europe, often breeds in nests of White Storks. Calls include a short, metallic 'chip' and 'chop', and a repeated 'chit-tchup'. Distinctive, liquid flight-call 'tek-tek' difficult to describe, but diagnostic once learnt. Found in woodland, farmland and scrub. Widespread but local.

Chaffinch *Fringilla coelebs* 15cm

male (above)
female (below)

A small, well-known finch. Adult male has back rich rufous-brown and tail blackish with conspicuous white outer feathers. Head and nape blue-grey, forecrown black. Wings dark brown with two white wingbars. Underparts rich pink, shading to white on lower belly. In winter, subdued due to buffish feather fringes. Female and immature brown above, pale fawn below with white-edged, dark brown tail. Brownish wings show two distinct wingbars. Often gregarious in winter. Call a ringing 'pink'. Song a rich, descending cascade, ending in a flourish. Occurs in all woodland types, farmland, parks, heaths and gardens. Widespread and common.

Brambling *Fringilla montifringilla* 15cm

This small, colourful finch, has a white rump. Summer adult male has head and back blackish, dark tail and white tail conspicuous in flight. Wings dark brown, orange forewing and white wingbar distinctive in flight. Throat and breast orange, shading to white on belly. Winter male has buff feather fringes obscuring the rich colours. Female and immature dark brown above with underparts orange-brown. Wingbar and white rump conspicuous in flight. Gregarious in winter. Call a flourishing 'tchway'. Song a series of 'twee' notes. Breeds in woodlands. Winters in woodland margins and farmland. Widespread but winter distribution and numbers variable.

Bullfinch *Pyrrhula pyrrhula* 15cm

A portly, heavy-bodied finch. Adult male has a black cap, dove-grey mantle and back. Striking white rump contrasts with black tail, best seen in flight. Underparts rich pink to crimson, shading to white on belly. Wings black, with single bold white wingbar. Female has black cap, grey-brown mantle, with back, rump, tail pattern and wing pattern as male. Underparts soft fawn. Immature similar to female, lacking black cap. Bill black and distinctively rounded. Call a distinctive, piping 'peeu'. Song, a quiet, creaking warble. Found in woodland, scrub, parks, hedges and gardens. Widespread but rarely numerous.

133

Hawfinch *Coccothraustes coccothraustes* 18cm

A large, robust finch with a massive bill. Adults of both sexes have chestnut head, brighter in male than female. Shows grey collar, rich brown back and rump, and relatively short, white-tipped tail. Head has black facial patch and bib and diagnostic, huge, silver-grey bill. Rest of underparts rich buff. Wings purplish-black, with bold white wingbar very conspicuous in deeply undulating flight. Secretive. Call a distinctive, explosive 'zik'. Song a subdued, Goldfinch-like twittering warble, seldom heard. Found in mature deciduous woodland, especially with hornbeam. Widespread but rarely numerous.

Serin *Serinus serinus* 10cm

A tiny, highly active finch. Adult male predominantly olive-green above, with dark streaks. Tail dark brown, contrasting with yellow rump, most noticeable in flight. Wings brown, with double yellow wingbars. Underparts bright yellow, shading to white on lower belly, with dark brown streaks on flanks. Bill small, stubby and triangular. Female and immature much duller above and almost white below, but also with bright yellow rump. Call a musical 'chur-lit'. Song a musical jingling, often delivered in song flight. Occurs in open woodland, parks and gardens with plentiful mature trees. Common in southern Europe. Rare vagrant to Britain.

Greenfinch *Carduelis chloris* 15cm

This small, greenish finch has a robust bill. Summer adult male olive-green above, with grey on nape and cheeks. Underparts largely rich yellow; wings brown, with bold yellow patches conspicuous in flight. Tail brown with yellow patches on either side of base. Winter adult brownish-olive, with less intense yellow patches in wings and tail. Immature similar to female, heavily streaked on back and flanks. Bill comparatively large, pale and triangular. Call a drawling 'dwee-ee'. Song an extended, purring trill, sometimes given in song flight. Occurs in open woodland, scrub, farmland, parks and gardens. Widespread and often numerous.

Siskin *Carduelis spinus* 12cm

A tiny, black and yellow finch. Adult male greenish-yellow above, often heavily streaked with black. Crown and small bib black, underparts yellow, shading to white on belly. Flanks streaked with brown, wings dark brown with double yellow wingbars. Yellow rump and yellow patches at sides of base of dark, forked tail, seen in flight. Female and immature duller, browner, with brown streaking. Bill dark, relatively long, pointed at tip. Gregarious in winter. Call, often during flight, a wheezy 'chwee-oo'. Song a prolonged twittering. Found in woodland, often conifers, but favours alder and birch in winter. Widespread and sometimes common.

Goldfinch *Carduelis carduelis* 13cm

A small, colourful finch. Adult unmistakable, with harlequin plumage. Black crown and nape contrast with red and white on face. In flight, broad gold wingbars distinctive, as is white rump, contrasting with black tail. Immature pale and buffer, with plain buff head. Bill whitish with dark tip. Relatively long and pointed for a finch. Call a distinctive, tinkling 'dee-dee-lit', particularly attractive when given by entire flocks. Song a prolonged, warbling twitter. Found on scrub and wasteground with abundant, seed-bearing weeds such as teasel. Also on farmland, open woodland, parks and gardens. Widespread and locally common.

Linnet *Carduelis cannabina* 13cm

A small, brown finch. Summer adult male attractive with rich chestnut back and reddish-pink on crown and breast. Head and underparts otherwise pale fawn, and wings brown with poorly defined white patch most easily seen in undulating flight. Shows whitish rump and white-edged black tail. Winter male, female and immature dull brown, paler below than above, lacking pink patches but often heavily streaked brown. Bill blackish and stubby. Gregarious outside breeding season. Call a penetrating 'tsweet'. Song a musical twittering, often given from prominent perch. Found on heaths, scrub and farmland. Widespread and locally common.

Redpoll *Carduelis flammea* 12cm

A small, rather dark finch. Adult has brown upperparts with blackish streaking. Underparts buffish, paling to white on belly. Shows small black bib and small red patch on forehead and crown. Male sometimes has pink flush on breast in summer. Immature duller, lacking bib and red on crown. Several geographical races: northern birds usually paler and slightly larger than southern ones. Call 'chee-chee-chit'. Song a distinctive, high-pitched purring trill, often delivered in circling song flight high above woodland. Occurs in mixed woodland, especially where birch is common. In winter, often mixes with Siskins. Fairly common.

Crossbill *Loxia curvirostra* 15cm

This small finch has a distinctive, cross-tipped bill. Adult male predominantly dull reddish or orange, with deeply forked, blackish tail. Wings blackish with no wingbars. Female and immature predominantly yellowish-olive, darker above than below with blackish streaking. Heavy parrot-like bill has crossed tips, used for extracting pine seeds from cones. Very agile in tree canopy when feeding. Often found in small flocks with females and immatures predominating. Call a loud and metallic 'jip'. Song a brief twittering. Occurs in coniferous woodland, usually spruce. Locally common. Sometimes populations irrupt westwards to areas outside normal range.

Corn Bunting *Miliaria calandra* 18cm

One of the larger European buntings, with a rather non-descript plumage. Looks plump-breasted, with dark sandy brown upperparts. Underparts paler sandy brown, paling to white on belly with copious brown streaks. Tail dark brown, lacking white outer feathers. Call a short 'tsrip' or disyllabic 'tsip-ip'. Song characteristic, a harsh, metallic jangling, often likened to jingling keys. Usually delivered from prominent songpost. A familiar sound in southern Europe. Occurs on open, dry farmland, areas of grassy heath and open scrub. Widespread, but precise distribution often patchy and numbers variable.

Reed Bunting *Emberiza schoeniclus* 15cm

A small, well-known bunting. Summer male back brown with darker streaks. Rump grey-brown, tail blackish with white outer feathers. Crown and face black with white collar running into white moustachial stripes. Underparts whitish with bold black throat and upper breast. In winter, pale feather fringes obscures pattern. Female and immature, brown above, buff below, with dark streaks on back and flanks. Brown crown separated from dark cheeks by buffish eye-stripe, with adjacent whitish and black moustachial stripes. Call 'tsee-you'. Song short, jangling and discordant. Found mainly in marshy areas, also dryish scrub. Widespread and often common.

Yellowhammer *Emberiza citrinella* 18cm

 A small, yellow bunting. Summer male back, rump and wings chestnut, streaked black and brown. Head and neck bright yellow, thin black marks on head. Breast and belly canary yellow, tinged chestnut on breast and flanks. Winter male browner, yellow obscured by buff fringes. Female and immature brown streaked above with chestnut rump. Head yellowish with dark streaking, underparts yellow, shading to white on belly. Streaked on flanks and breast. Tail dark with white outer feathers. Call a sharp 'twick'. Song a series of 'zit' notes, usually ending in wheezy 'zeee'. Occurs in hedgerows, scrub and heaths. Widespread and often common.

Snow Bunting *Plectrophenax nivalis* 17cm

 A small, strikingly pale bunting. Summer male mostly white, with black back, black and white wings, and black centre to tail. Winter male has ginger shading on crown and nape, and back mottled brown and buff. Female and immature mottled ginger brown above, with plain brown cap. Underparts fawn, shaded ginger on flanks and breast. In flight, black-tipped white wings characteristic. Call a plaintive 'teeu' or strident 'tsweet'. Song a rapid and musical twittering. Breeds on Arctic tundra and moors. In winter, found on coastal marshes and beaches. Locally common on breeding grounds. In winter, distribution and numbers irregular.

Further reading

Campbell, B. and Lack, E. (Eds), *A Dictionary of Birds*. T. & A.D. Poyser, Calton, 1985

Cramp, S. and Simmonds, K.E.L. (Eds), *Handbook of the Birds of Europe, the Middle East and North Africa*. Oxford University Press, Oxford, 1977 – (vols. I–V published to date)

Flegg, J. and Hosking, D., *Photographic Field Guide to Birds of Britain and Europe*. New Holland, London, 1993

Harrison, P., *Seabirds – An Identification Guide*. Croom Helm, London, 1985

Lack, P. (Ed), *The Atlas of Wintering Birds in Britain and Ireland*. T & A.D. Poyser, Calton, 1986

Madge, S., & Burn, H., *Wildfowl: An Identification Guide to the Ducks, Geese and Swans of the World*. Christopher Helm, London, 1988

Sterry, P.R., *Field Guide to the Birds of Britain and Europe*. The Crowood Press, Marlborough, 1994

Useful addresses

British Trust for Ornithology (BTO)
The Nunnery, Nunnery Place, Thetford, Norfolk IP24 2PU

English Nature
Northminster House, Peterborough, PE1 1UA

International Council for Bird Preservation (ICBP)
32 Cambridge Road, Girton, Cambridge CB3 0PJ

National Trust
36 Queen Anne's Gate, London SW1H 9AS

National Trust for Scotland
5 Charlotte Square, Edinburgh EH2 4DU

Royal Society for the Protection of Birds (RSPB)
The Lodge, Sandy, Beds SG19 2DL

Scottish Ornithologists' Club
21 Regent Terrace, Edinburgh EH7 5BT

Wildfowl and Wetlands Trust
Gatehouse, Slimbridge, Glos GL2 7BT

Index